Weight Watchers
IN THE UK
35 Year Anniversary 1967-2002

35 *years of*
Weight Watchers
favourite recipes

SIMON & SCHUSTER
A VIACOM COMPANY

Edited by Joy Skipper

First published in Great Britain by Simon & Schuster UK Ltd, 2002.
A Viacom Company.

Copyright © 2002, Weight Watchers International, Inc.

Simon & Schuster UK Ltd.
Africa House
64–78 Kingsway
London WC2B 6AH

Weight Watchers and *Pure Points* are Trademarks
of Weight Watchers International, Inc. and used under its
control by Weight Watchers (UK) Ltd.

Photography: Iain Bagwell
Styling: Rachel Jukes
Food preparation: Penny Stephens
Design: Jane Humphrey
Typesetting: Stylize Digital Artwork
Printed and bound in China

Weight Watchers Publications Manager: Corrina Griffin
Weight Watchers Publications Executive: Lucy Davidson
Weight Watchers Recipe Researcher: Tracey White

A CIP catalogue record for this book is available from the British Library.

ISBN 0 743 23091 4

Pictured on the back cover: Sticky Cinnamon Buns, page 63
Pictured on the title page: Chocolate Apricot Cheesecake, page 42

Raw eggs: Only the freshest eggs should be used. Pregnant women, the elderly and
children should avoid recipes with eggs which are raw or not fully cooked.

V denotes a vegetarian recipe and assumes vegetarian cheese and free-range eggs are
    used. Virtually fat-free fromage frais and low-fat crème fraîche may contain traces of
    gelatine so they are not always vegetarian: please check the labels.
(Vg) denotes a vegan dish.

Recipe notes: Egg size is medium unless otherwise stated. Fruit and vegetables are medium
size unless otherwise stated.

Recipe timings are approximate and meant to be guidelines. The preparation time includes
all the steps up to and following the main cooking time(s).

contents

celebrating
35 years
of Weight Watchers

35 years ago the first Weight Watchers Meeting was opened in the UK. It was such a unique and yet simple method of weight loss that it soon became a roaring success. People were finding that by simply following the healthy eating plan and attending weekly discussion groups, it was possible to lose weight and maintain that weight loss without ever feeling deprived, hungry or bored! In fact, people found that with Weight Watchers it was just the opposite! The Meetings were interesting and fun, the Members were introduced to tasty and filling low-fat foods, and yet they looked and felt better than ever! It really was a true recipe for success.

Three years later in 1970, the first Weight Watchers cookbook was published in the UK – and the rest, as they say, is history! Since then, Weight Watchers has been bringing you delicious and filling low-fat recipes, which have helped millions of Members throughout the UK to lose weight.

This book celebrates Weight Watchers 35 year anniversary in the UK, by bringing you the ultimate collection of favourite recipes from the first cookbook in 1970 up to the present day! There are lots of classic recipes and old favourites from the past, but you'll notice that we've often updated them slightly to include new and exciting ingredients that were not available to us all those years ago!

All the recipes in this book were chosen by Weight Watchers Leaders, Area Service Managers and Regional Managers – and what a fantastic job they have done! The book is a wonderful collection of delicious dishes that have helped all of them, individually, to lose weight and become the people that they are today. So, a big 'Thank You' to everyone who wrote in with their favourite Weight Watchers recipes from years gone by and amazed us again and again with fantastic suggestions for this book.

Our lifestyles have all changed since the first Weight Watchers cookbooks were published, and the last thing we want after a long day at work is to slave over a hot stove! With this in mind, the recipes are all easy to prepare and will not leave you tied to the kitchen for too long. Easy steps guide you to a perfect meal or snack in no time at all! This book will help you to stick to a healthy and nutritious, not to mention delicious, way of eating, with the added bonus that all the recipes are low in points to help you to look and feel great! So be inspired and get cooking!

Thank you to the following people for all their excellent recipe recommendations:
Anne Booth, Janet Carney, Linda Clifton, Jackie Cowie, Margaret Crawford, Heather David, Sally Debenham, Vivienne Elman, Janet Gaines, Sandra Hall, Sandra Handley, Sue Hughes, Louise Iles, Jacqui Johnson, Carol Jones, Kathryn Kendrick, Mo Kennedy, Jan Leach, Anja Leeves, Maggie Logan, Jan Matthews, Sheena McKee, Kathleen Moss, Mary Olsen, Debbie Orr, Mary Osborne, Sylvia Palmer, Helen Perry, Jane Prescott, Linda Robinson, Lynne Senior, Daya Stafford, Fiona Walker, Lynda Warlow, Marilyn Webb, Tracey White, Berendina Williams, Debbie Williams, Lesley Williams and Christine Younger.

light meals & snacks

Here are lots of ideas for tasty light meals and snacks – they're ideal for lunch or for when you want something satisfying but don't want to use up too many points. Some recipes are perfect for a snack at work and others are great for sharing with friends.

SPINACH AND POTATO GRATIN

POINTS

per recipe: 29   per serving: 7½

v Serves 4
Preparation time: 40 minutes
Cooking time: 40–50 minutes
Calories per serving: 460
Freezing: not recommended

This recipe was recommended by Jane Prescott, from Lincoln. It was originally published in 1993 and it's one of her all-time favourites.

750 g (1 lb 10 oz) potatoes, peeled and sliced about 5 mm (¼-inch) thick

750 g (1 lb 10 oz) fresh spinach, washed well

2 teaspoons olive oil

250 g (9 oz) half-fat mature Cheddar cheese, grated

350 g (12 oz) tomatoes, sliced

2 eggs

150 ml (5 fl oz) low-fat plain yogurt

salt and freshly ground black pepper

1 Preheat the oven to Gas Mark 4/ 180°C/fan oven 160°C. Cook the potatoes in a large pan of boiling salted water for 5 minutes then drain.

2 Pack the spinach into a very large pan and add a little salted water. Cover with a lid and cook for 4–5 minutes, by which time the spinach will have wilted.

3 Drain the spinach well, to make it as dry as possible, squeezing out any excess liquid with the back of a spoon.

4 Use the olive oil to grease a large, shallow ovenproof dish. Layer half the potatoes over the base, and season to taste. Sprinkle with half the cheese then cover with the spinach. Top with the remaining potatoes and, finally, a layer of sliced tomatoes.

5 Scatter the rest of the cheese evenly over the surface. Beat together the eggs and yogurt with some salt and pepper. Pour this mixture carefully over the cheese then bake for 40–50 minutes or until golden.

TOP TIP Use low-fat cooking spray instead of the olive oil and save ½ a point per serving.

Spinach and
potato gratin:
A tasty and
filling lunch.

Mediterranean vegetable salad: Incredibly fresh and flavourful.

MEDITERRANEAN VEGETABLE SALAD

POINTS

per recipe: 5½   per serving: 3

ⓥ Serves 2
Preparation and cooking time: 20 minutes
Calories per serving: 250
Freezing: not recommended

This recipe was recommended by Linda Clifton, a Diamond Leader from Wokingham. Linda finds this recipe really versatile – it's great as a packed lunch or with a barbecue.

½ yellow pepper, de-seeded and cut into large chunks

1 small courgette, sliced thickly

1 small onion or shallot, sliced

2 teaspoons olive oil

2 tomatoes, quartered and de-seeded

2 olives in brine, stoned and sliced

3 tablespoons fat-free vinaigrette dressing

½ teaspoon chilli sauce

½ teaspoon dried mixed herbs

300 g (10½ oz) cooked pasta

6 fresh basil leaves, torn

salt and freshly ground black pepper

1 Toss the pepper, courgette, onion or shallot and the olive oil in a large bowl. Heat a large, non-stick frying pan. When it is very hot, stir-fry the vegetables for 3–4 minutes, until they begin to soften and brown. Remove the pan from the heat.
2 Add the tomatoes and olives to the vegetable mixture.
3 Mix the vinaigrette dressing with the chilli sauce and the herbs. Season to taste and drizzle over the vegetables.
4 Fold the pasta and basil leaves into the vegetable mix, then divide between two bowls or containers. Cover and chill until required.

TOP TIP Use low-fat cooking spray instead of the olive oil and save 1 point per serving.

VARIATION This would be equally delicious if you replaced the pasta with 300 g (10½ oz) of cooked rice. The points will be 4 per serving.

SMOKY QUICHE

POINTS

per recipe: 36   per serving: 4½

Serves 8
Preparation time: 15 minutes
Cooking time: 25–30 minutes
Calories per serving: 200
Freezing: recommended

This recipe comes from a 1992 publication and was recommended by Louise Iles. Louise has been a member for 13 years and has lost five stone on the Programme.

20 cm (8-inch) cooked shortcrust pastry case

1 tablespoon olive oil

110 g (4 oz) onion, chopped finely

25 g (1 oz) lean back bacon, grilled and chopped

110 g (4 oz) curd cheese

60 g (2 oz) smoked cheese, grated

2 eggs, beaten

1 Preheat the oven to Gas Mark 5/ 190°C/fan oven 170°C. Place the pastry case on a baking sheet.
2 Heat the oil in a small saucepan. Add the onion and stir-fry for 2 minutes, cover and leave over a low heat for 5 minutes, until cooked.
3 Mix together the onion, bacon, and curd cheese in a bowl. Stir in the smoked cheese and eggs.
4 Spoon the egg and cheese mixture into the pastry case. Bake for 25–30 minutes or until the mixture is set. Serve hot or leave until cold then cut into wedges.

Smoky quiche: Losing weight is easy when low-point food tastes this good!

SPANISH TOMATO RICE

POINTS

per recipe: 25½   per serving: 6½

Ⓥ *Serves 4*

Preparation and cooking time: 40 minutes

Calories per serving: 410

Freezing: not recommended

This rice dish was suggested by Jackie Cowie, who joined Weight Watchers in 1991 in Middlesbrough, and lost 25 lbs to reach Goal. She is now a Leader in Aberdeen, and runs seven meetings a week. She says that this recipe is great eaten hot or cold!

1 tablespoon olive oil

1 onion, chopped

2 garlic cloves, crushed

1 red pepper, de-seeded and chopped

1 courgette, chopped

1 teaspoon chilli powder

1 teaspoon turmeric

225 g (8 oz) long-grain rice

450 ml (16 fl oz) vegetable stock

4 tablespoons dry white wine

400 g can of chopped tomatoes

175 g (6 oz) canned black-eyed beans

90 g (3¼ oz) frozen peas or petits pois

1 tablespoon fresh sage, chopped, or 2 teaspoons dried sage

salt and freshly ground black pepper

60 g (2 oz) Parmesan cheese, grated finely, to serve

1 Heat the oil in a large frying pan and stir-fry the onion and garlic for 3–4 minutes, until softened. Add the pepper and courgette and stir-fry for 2 more minutes.

2 Stir in the chilli, turmeric, and rice, and stir-fry for 2–3 minutes. Then add the stock, wine, tomatoes and black-eyed beans. Bring to the boil then reduce the heat, cover and simmer for 10 minutes.

3 Stir in the peas or petit pois, sage and seasoning. Simmer for another 5 minutes or until the rice is tender. Sprinkle with the cheese then serve immediately.

TOP TIPS If the rice becomes dry during cooking, add some more stock or water.

Use low-fat cooking spray instead of the olive oil and save ½ a point per serving.

Leave out the Parmesan cheese and save 2 points per serving.

Tandori chicken: Each delicious kebab is just 1½ points!

TANDOORI CHICKEN

POINTS

per recipe: 5½   per kebab: 1½

Serves 4

Preparation time: 20 minutes + 30 minutes marinating

Cooking time: 15 minutes

Calories per serving: 100

Freezing: not recommended

Linda Clifton suggested that this recipe be included in this book. Linda thinks that this recipe is 'ideal on the barbecue, as chicken pieces or a whole breast'. Serve with lemon wedges and some yogurt mixed with mint, adding the extra points.

1 garlic clove, crushed

1 teaspoon chilli powder

1 teaspoon paprika

½ teaspoon cumin seeds or ground cumin

½ teaspoon ground ginger

1 tablespoon lemon juice

1 tablespoon low-fat plain yogurt

½ teaspoon salt

350 g (12 oz) chicken breast, skinned and boned, cut into cubes

1 In a non-metallic bowl, mix together all the ingredients except the chicken.

2 Stir in the cubes of chicken. Cover the bowl then place in the fridge to marinate for at least 30 minutes (or overnight).

3 Thread the chicken on to four skewers, or wooden kebab sticks pre-soaked in water to prevent them from burning.

4 Place the skewers or kebab sticks on a barbecue or under a medium-hot grill. Cook for 12–15 minutes, turning frequently and basting with the remaining marinade.

Spanish tomato rice: Looks great, tastes amazing.

family favourites

Hearty casseroles, crusty pies and simple fish dishes make this a perfect chapter for the whole family to enjoy. All the recipes use easy to find ingredients, and once the dish is in the oven, you can take some time to relax before your meal. These family favourites can be served with low or zero point vegetables, to make a filling, tasty meal.

CARIBBEAN CHICKEN

POINTS

per recipe: 12   per serving: 6

Serves 2

Preparation time: cooking rice + 20 minutes

Cooking time: 1 hour

Calories per serving: 435

Freezing: not recommended

We couldn't believe the number of people who wrote in to recommend this dish! It seems to be a firm favourite with everyone.

2 × 150 g (5½ oz) skinless chicken breasts

1 teaspoon olive oil

1 onion, chopped

½ green pepper, chopped

2 teaspoons cornflour

2 canned pineapple rings, no sugar added, with 2 tablespoons juice

300 ml (½ pint) chicken stock

2 teaspoons tomato ketchup

2 teaspoons curry powder

salt and freshly ground pepper

TO SERVE

1 banana

175 g (6 oz) hot, cooked rice

1 Preheat the oven to Gas Mark 4/ 180°C/fan oven 160°C. Brown the chicken breasts in a large, non-stick frying pan then place them in a large, ovenproof dish.

2 Heat the oil in the non-stick pan you browned the chicken in then lightly fry the onion and pepper. Add them to the chicken.

3 Blend the cornflour with the pineapple juice. Pour the stock into the frying-pan then add the pineapple rings, cornflour mixture, ketchup, curry powder and seasoning. Bring the mixture to the boil then pour it over the chicken.

4 Bake for 1 hour or until the chicken is cooked.

5 Slice the banana in half lengthways. Cut it into pieces and stir into the mixture just before serving. Divide the sauce into two equal portions and serve with the rice.

TOP TIP Use low-fat cooking spray instead of the olive oil and save ½ a point per serving.

Caribbean chicken:
A real treat for
family and friends!

Boston beef
and baked
bean hotpot:
Incredibly
satisfying for
only 6 points
per serving.

BOSTON BEEF AND BAKED BEAN HOTPOT

POINTS

per recipe: 24	per serving: 6

Serves 4
Preparation time: 20 minutes
Cooking time: 40 minutes
Calories per serving: 385
Freezing: recommended

This tasty dish was suggested by Fiona Walker, an Area Service Manager from Bedford. She was still a Leader when the recipe was first published, and says 'it became so popular in my meetings that it almost had a "cult" following'.

350 g (12 oz) extra-lean minced beef
2 teaspoons vegetable oil
2 onions, chopped
300 ml (½ pint) beef stock
225 g (8 oz) canned plum tomatoes
415 g can of baked beans
110 g (4 oz) pasta shapes, such as spirals
2 teaspoons Worcestershire sauce
2 teaspoons tomato purée
2 teaspoons barbecue sauce
a pinch of dried herbs
salt and freshly ground black pepper
chopped parsley, to garnish

1 Sauté the minced beef in a large, non-stick frying pan for 4–5 minutes, until browned. Drain off the fat.

2 Heat the oil in a large saucepan then gently cook the onions, until soft. Stir in the mince along with all the remaining ingredients, except the parsley. Bring to the boil then reduce the heat and simmer, covered, for 40 minutes, until the meat and pasta are cooked and tender.

3 Check the seasoning then sprinkle with lots of fresh chopped parsley before serving.

TOP TIP Use low-fat cooking spray instead of the vegetable oil and save ½ a point per serving.

HUNGARIAN BEEF CASSEROLE

POINTS

per recipe: 21½	per serving: 5½

Serves 4
Preparation time: 30 minutes
Cooking time: 1½ hours
Calories per serving: 400
Freezing: recommended

Jackie Cowie, who suggested this dish, joined Weight Watchers 10 years ago, and has been a Leader in Teeside for eight years. It's easy to prepare and the result is absolutely delicious – fantastic as a winter warmer!

2 teaspoons vegetable oil
350 g (12 oz) very lean stewing steak, cubed
1 large onion, sliced
1 garlic clove, crushed
2 tablespoons paprika
400 g can of chopped tomatoes
1 tablespoon tomato purée
1 red pepper, de-seeded and chopped
1 yellow pepper, de-seeded and chopped
1 courgette, sliced
1 beef stock cube, dissolved in 450 ml (16 fl oz) hot water
1 tablespoon cornflour, blended with a little cold water
salt and freshly ground black pepper

FOR THE MASH

850 g (1 lb 13 oz) potatoes, peeled and cubed
1 tablespoon skimmed milk

TO SERVE

4 tablespoons low-fat plain yogurt
paprika, for sprinkling
fresh parsley, chopped

1 Heat the oil in a large saucepan until it is very hot. Add the steak a handful at a time and cook for 5–7 minutes, to seal and brown the meat – try not to crowd the pan as the meat will start to steam. Turn the heat down a little then add the onion and garlic. Cook, stirring, for about 3 minutes, until softened. Add the paprika and stir well to coat the steak and onions.

2 Add the tomatoes, tomato purée, red and yellow peppers, courgette and stock to the pan. Bring to the boil then reduce the heat, cover and simmer for 1½ hours or until the meat is very tender. Check the level of liquid from time to time, adding a little extra water if necessary.

3 During the last 25 minutes, cook the potatoes in lightly salted boiling water, until tender. Mash them well with the milk, and beat until smooth.

4 Season the casserole to taste then stir in the blended cornflour. Cook for a couple of minutes, until the sauce thickens.

5 Divide the casserole between four plates then top each portion with 1 tablespoon of yogurt and sprinkle with paprika and chopped parsley. Serve with the mashed potatoes.

TOP TIP Use low-fat cooking spray instead of the vegetable oil and save ½ a point per serving.

PORK WITH MUSHROOM, MUSTARD AND TARRAGON SAUCE

POINTS

per recipe: 20½   **per serving: 5**

Serves 4
Preparation and cooking time: 20 minutes
Calories per serving: 295
Freezing: not recommended

This recipe was suggested by Jan Matthews, an Area Service Manager from Lancashire. With its light and creamy sauce, this recipe really is delicious.

2 teaspoons olive or sunflower oil

4 × 150 g (5½ oz) lean pork steaks

1 onion, chopped finely

250 g (9 oz) mixed mushrooms (e.g. chestnut, oyster, open-cap), sliced

4 tablespoons dry white wine

1 tablespoon whole-grain mustard

125 ml (4 fl oz) half-fat crème fraîche

2 tablespoons fresh tarragon, chopped or 1 teaspoon dried tarragon

salt and freshly ground black pepper

1 Heat the oil in a large, non-stick frying pan. Fry the pork steaks for 3–4 minutes on each side or until browned and cooked through. Remove from the pan with a slotted spoon and keep warm.

2 Add the onion and mushrooms to the pan and fry for 3–4 minutes or until softened. Pour the wine over and allow it to bubble and reduce by half. Stir in the mustard, crème fraîche and tarragon, and season well.

3 Return the pork steaks to the pan, along with any juices. Bring to the boil, simmer for 1 minute, then serve.

OPEN CRUST CHICKEN AND MUSHROOM PIE

POINTS

per recipe: 23½   **per serving: 4**

Serves 6
Preparation time: 35 minutes + 30 minutes chilling
Cooking time: 50 minutes
Calories per serving: 220
Freezing: not recommended

Jane Prescott, an Area Service Manager from Lincoln, and Louise Iles, a Member from Weston-Super-Mare, suggested this recipe. For a vegetarian alternative, Jane recommends replacing the chicken with Quorn. The points will remain the same.

FOR THE PASTRY

110 g (4 oz) plain white flour

pinch of salt

60 g (2 oz) polyunsaturated margarine

2 tablespoons plain white flour, for rolling

FOR THE FILLING

1 teaspoon sunflower oil

175 g (6 oz) skinless, boneless chicken breast, diced

1 onion, chopped

1 garlic clove, crushed

110 g (4 oz) closed-cup mushrooms, sliced

4 tomatoes, peeled and chopped

2 tablespoons tomato purée

1 large courgette, chopped

1 tablespoon fresh tarragon, chopped or 1 teaspoon dried tarragon

1 egg, separated

15 g (½ oz) semolina

1 teaspoon Parmesan cheese, grated

salt and freshly ground black pepper

1 To make the pastry, sift the flour and salt into a large bowl then lightly rub in the margarine until the mixture resembles fine breadcrumbs. Using a blunt-ended knife, stir in enough ice-cold water – about 3 or 4 tablespoons – to form a soft, but not sticky, dough. Knead the dough lightly until smooth. Place it in a polythene bag then chill for 30 minutes in the refrigerator.

2 To make the filling, heat the oil in a medium-size, non-stick frying pan and cook the chicken, onion and garlic for 5 minutes over a medium heat. Add the mushrooms, tomatoes, tomato purée, courgette, tarragon and seasoning, and simmer gently for 15 minutes.

3 Preheat the oven to Gas Mark 6/ 200°C/fan oven 180°C. Roll out the chilled pastry on a lightly floured surface to form a rough 25 cm (10-inch) circle. Place it on a floured baking sheet.

4 Brush the pastry with egg yolk and sprinkle over the semolina. Spoon the chicken and mushroom filling over, leaving a 4 cm (1½-inch) border all around. Turn the edges of the pastry in to cover part of the filling.

5 Brush the folded-over pastry with egg white then sprinkle with the Parmesan cheese. Bake the pie for 30–35 minutes, until golden.

Open crust chicken and mushroom pie: Only 4 points for each scrumptious slice!

Spicy mince
tortillas: Terrific
tortillas for only
6 points!

SPICY MINCE TORTILLAS

POINTS

per recipe: 11½	per serving: 6

ⓥ if following variation

Serves 2
Preparation time: 20 minutes
Cooking time: 20 minutes
Calories per serving: 405
Freezing: recommended

This recipe was recommended by Mo Kennedy, a Leader from Bedford. Mo says that this dish is quick and economic to make and is so simple.

2 teaspoons olive oil
½ small onion, chopped
2 garlic cloves, crushed
½ yellow pepper, de-seeded and chopped
½ courgette, chopped
110 g (4 oz) extra-lean minced beef
2 teaspoons mild curry paste
½ teaspoon turmeric
225 g (8 oz) canned chopped tomatoes
15 g (½ oz) raisins
salt and freshly ground black pepper

TO SERVE
2 medium-size soft flour tortillas
4 tablespoons low-fat plain yogurt

1 Heat the oil in a large frying pan and cook the onion, garlic and pepper for 5 minutes. Add the courgette and cook for another 4 minutes.
2 Meanwhile, brown the mince in a medium-size, non-stick pan and drain off any excess fat.
3 Add the mince to the vegetables and stir in the curry paste, turmeric, tomatoes, 4 tablespoons of water and the raisins. Bring to the boil and then reduce the heat. Simmer gently for 15 minutes. Season to taste. Preheat the oven to Gas Mark 5/190°C/fan oven 170°C.
4 While the meat mixture is cooking, wrap the tortillas in foil and place them in the preheated oven until warm, about 3–4 minutes.
5 Divide the mince between the tortillas. Top each with two tablespoons of yogurt and serve.

VARIATION For a delicious vegetarian version use minced Quorn instead of beef. Omit step 2 and add the Quorn with the ingredients in step 3. This will reduce the points to 4½ per serving. To reduce the points further use low-fat cooking spray instead of olive oil. This saves an extra ½ point per serving.

SALMON WITH SUN-DRIED TOMATO COUSCOUS

POINTS

per recipe: 32	per serving: 8

Serves 4
Preparation and cooking time: 30 minutes + 50 minutes standing time
Calories per serving: 515
Freezing: not recommended

Published in 2000, this recipe has established itself as a favourite for Linda Clifton and her husband.

50 g (1¾ oz) sun-dried tomatoes
225 g (8 oz) couscous
a pinch of garlic salt
1 teaspoon balsamic vinegar
1 tablespoon olive oil
4 × 150 g (5½ oz) salmon fillets
2 tablespoons fresh basil leaves, torn
salt and freshly ground black pepper

1 Place the sun-dried tomatoes in a small dish then pour 300 ml (½ pint) of boiling water over them. Cover and leave them to soak for 30 minutes. When soaked, drain the tomatoes, reserving the liquid, and chop them very finely.
2 Place the couscous in a bowl and stir in the chopped sun-dried tomatoes, garlic salt and balsamic vinegar. Put the reserved tomato liquid in a small pan and bring to the boil. Pour it over the couscous. Fluff the couscous up with a fork then cover the bowl with clingfilm. Leave it to stand for 20 minutes, fluffing it up again halfway through.
3 Heat the oil in a griddle pan or large, heavy-based frying pan. Rinse the salmon fillets then pat them dry with absorbent kitchen towel. Season them well with pepper then place them in the pan, skin-side down. Cook for 5 minutes. Carefully turn them over and cook for 1–2 more minutes, until just cooked through.
4 Toss the basil into the couscous mixture then season to taste. Divide the couscous between four serving plates, top with a salmon fillet and serve hot.

Salmon with sun-dried tomato couscous: Simply yummy!

LAMB JALFREZI

POINTS

per recipe: 29   per serving: 7½

Serves 4
Preparation time: 30 minutes
Cooking time: 50 minutes
Calories per serving: 215
Freezing: recommended

Debbie Orr, an Area Service Manager from Staffordshire, recommended this recipe. She says 'The taste is really authentic. Take-away night on Fridays becomes a treat'.

400 g (14 oz) lean stewing lamb (leg shank or neck fillet), trimmed of fat and diced
1 teaspoon cumin seeds
2 teaspoons sunflower oil
1 onion, sliced thinly
2 garlic cloves, chopped finely
2 cm (¾-inch) piece of fresh root ginger, grated
1 large green chilli, de-seeded and chopped
1 teaspoon paprika
½ teaspoon hot chilli powder
½ teaspoon ground turmeric
1 red pepper, de-seeded and sliced
1 small yellow pepper, de-seeded and sliced
4 tomatoes, skinned and chopped
150 ml (¼ pint) vegetable stock
2 tablespoons chopped fresh coriander
salt and freshly ground black pepper

1 Preheat the oven to Gas Mark 4/ 180°C/fan oven 160°C. Heat a large, non-stick frying pan and brown the lamb on all sides for about 5 minutes. Transfer to a medium-size casserole dish.

2 Sprinkle the cumin seeds into the pan and cook for a few seconds to release their aroma. Add the oil, onion, garlic, ginger and chilli. Stir and cook gently for 3 minutes. Mix in the paprika, hot chilli powder and turmeric. Cook for another minute.

3 Add the sliced peppers and chopped tomatoes, and continue cooking for 5 minutes, until they have softened. Add the stock towards the end of the 5 minutes. Season well then pour the sauce over the lamb.

4 Put the lid on the casserole and bake for about 50 minutes, or until the lamb is tender. Stir in the chopped coriander before serving.

RICH RED CHICKEN WITH ROSEMARY AND CHERRY TOMATOES

POINTS

per recipe: 13   per serving: 3½

Serves 4
Preparation time: 50 minutes
Cooking time: 50 minutes
Calories per serving: 245
Freezing: recommended

Linda Clifton and Mo Kennedy suggested this recipe, first published in 1998.

4 onions, quartered
4 teaspoons olive oil
300 g (10½ oz) part-boned, skinless chicken breasts
2 garlic cloves, crushed
3 teaspoons fresh rosemary, chopped
2 tablespoons sun-dried tomato paste
100 ml (3½ fl oz) red wine
2 teaspoons plain white flour
450 ml (16 fl oz) chicken stock
350 g (12 oz) small, flat mushrooms
2 tablespoons whole-grain mustard
225 g (8 oz) cherry tomatoes
salt and freshly ground black pepper
flat leaf parsley leaves, to garnish

1 Preheat the oven to Gas Mark 4/ 180°C/fan oven 160°C. Heat a large, non-stick frying pan until hot. Add the onions with 2 teaspoons of oil. Reduce the heat and cook for 10 minutes, stirring, until the onions are just beginning to soften and turn golden. Using a slotted spoon, transfer them to a large casserole dish with a tight-fitting lid.

2 Add the remaining oil and chicken to the pan. Cook on one side for 5 minutes, until the meat seals and colours slightly. Add the garlic and rosemary then turn the breasts over and cook for 5 more minutes, to seal them. Transfer the chicken to the casserole dish.

3 Stir the sun-dried tomato paste and wine into the garlic and rosemary. Cook for 3–4 minutes to reduce the liquid slightly then blend in the flour. Cook, stirring, for 3–4 more minutes, until smooth. Stir in the stock. Bring it all to the boil then pour it over the chicken. Cover the casserole dish and bake for 50 minutes.

4 Meanwhile, wipe out the frying pan with absorbent kitchen towel. Dry-fry the mushrooms over a gentle heat, until they begin to soften and release a little moisture. Continue to cook gently for 5 minutes.

5 Stir the mushrooms, mustard and tomatoes into the casserole. Season to taste. Return to the oven, uncovered, for 10 minutes, or until the tomatoes are just tender. Serve, garnished with parsley leaves.

TUNA, COURGETTE AND LEEK LASAGNE

POINTS

per recipe: 22   per serving: 5½

Serves 4
Preparation time: 40 minutes
Cooking time: 35 minutes
Calories per serving: 400
Freezing: recommended

From a 1995 publication, this recipe offers a wonderful alternative to traditional lasagne. Linda Clifton, a Diamond Leader who runs three meetings a week, says 'it's tasty, easy to make and the portion size is very substantial.'

---

2 teaspoons vegetable oil

1 onion, chopped

2 garlic cloves, crushed

1 leek, chopped finely

400 g (14 oz) canned chopped tomatoes

2 tablespoons tomato purée

2 courgettes, halved lengthways and sliced

1 teaspoon dried oregano

240 g (8½ oz) canned tuna in brine, drained and flaked

110 g (4 oz) no pre-cook lasagne sheets

110 g (4 oz) half-fat mature Cheddar cheese, grated

salt and freshly ground black pepper

FOR THE WHITE SAUCE

4 teaspoons polyunsaturated margarine

25 g (1 oz) plain white flour

300 ml (½ pint) skimmed milk

1 teaspoon English mustard

salt and freshly ground black pepper

---

1 Preheat the oven to Gas Mark 5/190°C/fan oven 170°C.

2 Heat the oil in a medium-size saucepan and cook the onion, garlic and leek for 5 minutes, or until softened. Stir in the tomatoes, tomato purée, courgettes and oregano. Bring to the boil then reduce the heat, cover the pan and simmer gently for 15 minutes.

3 Meanwhile, prepare the white sauce. Melt the margarine in a small saucepan, stir in the flour then cook for 1 minute. Gradually whisk in the milk and cook, whisking continuously, until the sauce thickens. Remove the pan from the heat, stir in the mustard and season well.

4 Mix the tuna and seasoning into the tomato sauce. Spoon half of the tomato mixture into a shallow, ovenproof dish then top with half of the lasagne sheets. Spread half of the white sauce over then sprinkle with half of the cheese. Repeat the layers in the same order to use up the remaining ingredients, finishing with a sprinkling of cheese.

5 Bake for 35 minutes, until bubbling and golden.

TOP TIP Use low-fat cooking spray instead of vegetable oil and save ½ a point per serving.

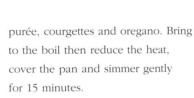

Tuna, courgette and leek lasagne: Delicious and filling for just 5½ points.

quick
& easy meals

If you're in a hurry and can't decide what to eat, this chapter will help you make up your mind! Most of the recipes take less than 30 minutes to cook, and all of them have lots of flavour and are low in points. What more could you want? When time is really short, why not try Chinese Lamb Stir-Fry (page 31) or Steak with Pepper and Spring Onions (page 28)? Some recipes can even be prepared ahead of time and frozen until you need a quick and easy meal.

TAGLIATELLE WITH SMOKED SALMON AND ASPARAGUS

POINTS	
per recipe: $18^{1}/_{2}$	per serving: $4^{1}/_{2}$

Serves 4
Preparation and cooking time: 25 minutes
Calories per serving: 350
Freezing: not recommended

This dish was proposed by Sandra Handley, an Area Service Manager from Middlesex. She says it's 'filling and tasty – we have it at least twice a month!'

110 g (4 oz) low-fat soft cheese
175 g (6 oz) smoked salmon trimmings
4 tablespoons dry white wine
1 teaspoon lemon juice
1 tablespoon chopped dill
225 g (8 oz) tagliatelle or linguine
350 g (12 oz) fresh asparagus, trimmed and cut into 5 cm (2-inch) pieces
salt and freshly ground black pepper
fresh dill sprigs, to garnish

1 Put the soft cheese, 60 g (2 oz) of the salmon trimmings, the wine and lemon juice into a liquidiser and process until smooth. Transfer to a small saucepan and heat through very gently. Do not allow the sauce to boil. Season to taste then stir in the chopped dill and remaining salmon trimmings.
2 Cook the pasta in plenty of lightly salted boiling water, according to the packet instructions. Drain thoroughly then return it to the warm saucepan.
3 Meanwhile, cook the asparagus in lightly salted boiling water for 5 minutes, until just tender. Drain the asparagus.
4 Add the sauce and the asparagus to the pasta and carefully fold everything together. Divide the pasta mixture between four warm plates, garnish with a piece of dill and serve immediately.

TOP TIP Ask for smoked salmon trimmings at the deli counter of your supermarket – they are much cheaper than slices.

VARIATION This dish is equally delicious using mange-tout peas, tiny broccoli florets or courgette matchsticks instead of asparagus.

Tagliatelle with smoked salmon and asparagus: Enjoy this satisfying pasta dish for only 4½ points!

Quick and easy
paella: Lots
of fantastic
ingredients and
only 4½ points
per serving!

QUICK AND EASY PAELLA

POINTS

per recipe: 18½   per serving: 4½

Serves 4
Preparation time: 15 minutes
Cooking time: 20 minutes + 5 minutes standing
Calories per serving: 340
Freezing: not recommended

This suggestion was put forward by Sally Debenham. Sally enjoys putting recipes from the cookbooks to the test and this is one of her all-time favourites.

2 teaspoons sunflower or olive oil
2 lean back bacon rashers, trimmed of fat and chopped
150 g (5½ oz) skinless, boneless chicken breast, chopped
1 onion, chopped
2 garlic cloves, crushed
1 small red pepper, de-seeded and chopped
1 tablespoon paprika
1 teaspoon turmeric
2 teaspoons dried marjoram
200 g (7 oz) risotto rice
850 ml (1½ pints) chicken stock
125 g (4½ oz) frozen peas, defrosted
salt and freshly ground black pepper

1 Heat the oil in a large, non-stick frying pan with a lid. Stir-fry the bacon and chicken for about 2 minutes then add the onion, garlic and red pepper.

2 Continue cooking for about 3 minutes, stirring occasionally. Mix in the paprika, turmeric, marjoram and rice and cook for 1 more minute.

3 Pour in the stock and bring to the boil, stirring well. It will look very wet, but don't worry – risotto rice absorbs a lot of liquid. Season to taste then turn the heat down to a simmer. Cover and cook gently for about 15 minutes or until all the liquid is absorbed. While it is cooking, stir or shake the pan once only.

4 Add the peas and cook for another 3 minutes.

5 Remove from the heat, cover and leave to stand for 5 minutes before serving.

TURKEY AND BROCCOLI PASTA WITH MUSTARD CRÈME FRAÎCHE

POINTS

per recipe: 16½   per serving: 4

Serves 4
Preparation and cooking time: 25 minutes
Calories per serving: 310
Freezing: not recommended

Linda Clifton suggested that this recipe should have a place in the 35 Years Cookbook. The recipe was originally published in 2000 – the same year that Linda became a Diamond Leader!

175 g (6 oz) dried pasta – such as fusilli, tagliatelle or spaghetti
275 g (9½ oz) broccoli, broken into florets
low-fat cooking spray
275 g (9½ oz) turkey breast strips
1 small onion, chopped
125 g (4½ oz) mushrooms, sliced
200 ml (7 fl oz) hot chicken stock
1 tablespoon Dijon mustard
2 teaspoons cornflour
4 tablespoons half-fat crème fraîche
salt and freshly ground black pepper

1 Cook the pasta in a large pan of boiling, salted water for 10 minutes. Halfway through the cooking time add the broccoli to the pan.

2 Meanwhile, spray a large, non-stick frying pan with low-fat cooking spray and cook the turkey, onion and mushrooms for 3–4 minutes. Pour in the hot stock and bring to the boil. Blend the mustard and cornflour with the crème fraîche and stir this mixture into the frying pan. Simmer for 5 minutes.

3 Thoroughly drain the pasta and broccoli then combine them with the turkey and sauce. Season well with plenty of black pepper. Divide between four warmed bowls and serve.

VARIATION Add a teaspoon of garlic purée to the turkey at step 2. The points per serving will be 4½.

STEAK WITH PEPPER AND SPRING ONIONS

POINTS

per recipe: 11½	per serving: 6

Serves 2
Preparation and cooking time: 15 minutes
Calories per serving:
Freezing: not recommended

Recommended by Mary Osborne, an Area Service Manager from Lancashire, this recipe was first written in 1993 and is a quick and easy treat!

175 g (6 oz) sirloin or fillet steak, about 2.5 cm (1-inch) thick
2 tablespoons olive oil
½ red or yellow pepper, de-seeded and cut into thin strips
1 bunch of spring onions cut into 2 cm (¾-inch) slices
½ teaspoon cornflour
5 tablespoons ginger wine
1–2 teaspoons lemon juice
salt and freshly ground black pepper

1 Lay the steak on a grill pan and cook it about 6 cm (2½ inches) from the heat for 7–8 minutes, turning once, until browned but rare.
2 Heat the oil in a saucepan then stir-fry the pepper and spring onions over a medium heat for 4 minutes.
3 Blend the cornflour with the ginger wine.
4 Transfer the steak to a chopping board and cut it into very thin slices.

Add the steak to the pepper and spring onions. Pour in the ginger wine mixture then cook over a very high heat, until the sauce is boiling and the steak is cooked to your liking.
5 Remove the saucepan from the heat and season to taste. Add lemon juice to taste and serve immediately.

TOP TIPS While the steak is cooking, put 90 g (3¼ oz) tagliatelle in salted, boiling water and cook for 8–10 minutes. Serve with the steak. This will add 2 points per serving.

If you want to reduce the points, use low-fat cooking spray instead of the olive oil and save 2½ points per serving.

Mexican stir-fry: Tastes fantastic.

MEXICAN STIR-FRY

POINTS

per recipe: 19½	per serving: 5

Ⓥ *Serves 4*
Preparation and cooking time: 30 minutes
Calories per serving: 475
Freezing: not recommended

Jackie Cowie, a Diamond Leader originally from Middlesbrough, but now in Aberdeen, proposed this recipe for the 35 Years Cookbook. First published in 1997, this dish is great to share with friends, as it's so simple to make!

1 tablespoon sunflower oil
1 red onion, quartered and sliced
2 garlic cloves, crushed
1 red pepper, de-seeded and chopped
1 yellow pepper, de-seeded and chopped
1 green pepper, de-seeded and chopped
1 teaspoon cayenne pepper
2 teaspoons cumin seeds
2 courgettes, chopped
3 tomatoes, chopped roughly
150 g (5½ oz) baby corn, halved
2 tablespoons fresh coriander leaves, chopped
salt and freshly ground black pepper

TO SERVE

8 medium-size soft flour tortillas
150 ml (5 fl oz) 0% fat Greek yogurt

1 Heat the oil in a large frying pan or wok then fry the onion, garlic and peppers for 3–4 minutes. Add the cayenne pepper and cumin seeds and cook for 2 minutes more. Preheat the oven to Gas Mark 5/190°C/fan oven 170°C.
2 Add the courgettes, tomatoes and corn and cook for a further 5–7 minutes. Stir in the coriander and seasoning. Spoon into a large serving dish.
3 Wrap the tortillas in foil and heat in the preheated oven for 3–4 minutes.
4 To serve, spoon some of the stir-fry mixture on to a warmed tortilla and top with a spoonful of Greek yogurt. Roll up the tortilla and eat with your fingers. Allow two tortillas per person.

TOP TIP Use low-fat cooking spray instead of the sunflower oil to reduce the points to 4½ per serving.

Steak with pepper and spring onions: Cook up a filling feast in no time at all!

1 Heat half the oil in a large, heavy-bottomed frying pan until quite hot then stir-fry the turkey for 2 minutes, until browned. Remove from the pan with a slotted spoon.

2 Heat the remaining oil then stir-fry the spring onions, carrot and pepper for 2 minutes. Add the rice and the curry powder. Cook for 1 more minute.

3 Pour in the stock and soy sauce. Return the meat to the pan, and bring it all to the boil, stirring continuously. Cover the pan, turn down the heat to a gentle simmer then cook for 15 minutes.

4 Check the seasoning and cook for a further 3–5 minutes, until all the liquid has been absorbed.

5 Stir in the parsley and serve on warm plates. Top with a tablespoon of yogurt and sprinkle with the toasted almonds.

TOP TIP To reduce the points to 7½ per serving use low-fat cooking spray instead of the sunflower oil.

VARIATION Substitute 350 g (12 oz) cooked green lentils or chick-peas for the turkey to make a vegetarian version of this pilaff. The points will be 9½ per serving.

Turkey and pepper pilaff: Quick and delicious – ideal for a midweek meal.

TURKEY AND PEPPER PILAFF

POINTS

per recipe: 17   per serving: 8½

ⓥ *if following variation*
Serves 2
Preparation and cooking time: 45 minutes
Calories per serving: 580
Freezing: recommended

Anja Leeves, an Area Service Manager from Uckfield in East Sussex, put this recipe forward as one of her favourite dishes. It is a vibrant, quick and delicious meal!

1 tablespoon sunflower oil
225 g (8 oz) skinless turkey breast, sliced or turkey stir-fry strips
2 spring onions, chopped
1 carrot, grated
1 green or yellow pepper, de-seeded and sliced
175 g (6 oz) easy-cook long-grain rice
1–2 teaspoons mild curry powder
600 ml (1 pint) chicken stock
1 tablespoon light soy sauce
2 tablespoons fresh parsley, chopped
salt and freshly ground black pepper

TO SERVE

2 tablespoons low-fat plain yogurt
15 g (½ oz) toasted flaked almonds

CHINESE LAMB STIR-FRY

POINTS

per recipe: 7½   per serving: 7½

Serves 1
Preparation and cooking time: 20 minutes
Calories per serving: 630
Freezing: not recommended

Janet Carney, a Leader from Lancashire, suggested this recipe. Janet says it's very quick and tasty. Whenever she asks her husband what he wants for tea, he says 'make that lamb thing' and she always knows what he means!

60 g (2 oz) spaghetti
90 g (3¼ oz) lean lamb stir-fry or boneless leg steak, trimmed of all fat and cut into thin strips
1 teaspoon sunflower oil
¼ small red pepper, de-seeded and sliced thinly
2 spring onions, sliced
1 carrot, cut into thin sticks
1 small courgette, cut into thin sticks
1 tablespoon dry sherry or vermouth (optional)
2 tablespoons light soy sauce
1 teaspoon sesame oil
1 teaspoon sesame seeds
salt and freshly ground black pepper

1 Break the spaghetti in half and cook in lightly salted boiling water, according to the packet instructions. Drain, rinse in cold water then set aside.

2 Heat a non-stick wok or heavy-based frying pan until quite hot then then stir-fry the lamb strips for about 2 minutes, until browned. Remove the lamb and keep it warm.

3 Add the oil to the wok or pan and heat it until quite hot. Add all the vegetables and stir-fry for about 2 minutes until just softened. Return the lamb to the wok.

4 Mix in the sherry or vermouth, if using, soy sauce and sesame oil. Heat until bubbling. Stir in the spaghetti and cook until hot.

5 Check the seasoning. Sprinkle over the sesame seeds then serve immediately.

TOP TIP Use low-fat cooking spray instead of the sunflower oil to reduce the points to 6½ per serving.

PAPRIKA BEAN CASSEROLE

POINTS

per recipe: 18   per serving: 4½

Ⓥ Serves 4
Preparation time: 15 minutes
Cooking time: 25 minutes
Calories per serving: 365
Freezing: recommended

This recipe was originally written for a 1995 cookbook and was put forward by Jane Prescott, an Area Service Manager from Lincoln. The recipe is a great, easy-to-prepare meal, and uses store cupboard ingredients, so it can be made at a moment's notice!

2 teaspoons sunflower or olive oil
2 large onions, sliced
1 garlic clove, crushed
400 g (14 oz) canned whole red pimientos, drained and chopped
350 g (12 oz) canned cannellini beans, rinsed and drained
2 tablespoons paprika
2 × 400 g cans chopped tomatoes
2 tablespoons tomato purée
225 g (8 oz) couscous

1 Heat the oil in a large saucepan then cook the onions and garlic for 5 minutes.

2 Stir in the pimientos, cannellini beans, paprika, tomatoes and tomato purée. Bring to the boil then cover and simmer for 25 minutes.

3 Meanwhile, cook the couscous according to packet instructions.

4 Spoon the couscous on to four serving plates, top with the bean casserole then serve immediately.

TOP TIP Use low-fat cooking spray instead of the sunflower or olive oil to reduce the points to 4 per serving.

vegetarian

These recipes show you how to turn vegetables into something really tasty. Using beans, pulses, pasta and a variety of fresh vegetables, the choice of curries, gratins, pies and bakes is endless. Even cooked one day and eaten the next, the Mushroom and Pepper Chilli (page 35) or Red Lentil and Vegetable Curry (page 38) are absolutely delicious.

RICH BEAN MOUSSAKA

POINTS

per recipe: **22½**   per serving: **5½**

V Serves 4
Preparation time: 50 minutes
Cooking time: 1 hour
Calories per serving: 360
Freezing: recommended

A firm favourite with both Charlotte Keys and Jacqui Johnson. This recipe was first published in 1995, and is delicious served with a crisp green salad.

5 teaspoons olive oil

1 large aubergine, sliced

1 large onion, chopped

2 garlic cloves, crushed

1 red pepper, de-seeded and chopped

400 g can chopped tomatoes

2 tablespoons tomato purée

220 g (7½ oz) canned red kidney beans, drained, rinsed and mashed gently

½ teaspoon ground cinnamon

4 tablespoons red wine

4 tablespoons cornflour

600 ml (1 pint) skimmed milk

110 g (4 oz) mature half-fat Cheddar cheese

1 egg

salt and freshly ground black pepper

1 Preheat the oven to Gas Mark 5/ 190°C/fan oven 170°C. Lightly grease a baking sheet with 1 teaspoon of oil. Place the aubergine slices on the sheet in one layer. Using a total of 3 teaspoons, brush the tops of the aubergine slices with oil. Bake in the oven for 20 minutes or until golden.

2 Meanwhile, heat the remaining teaspoon of oil in a saucepan then cook the onion, garlic and red pepper for 5 minutes, until softened. Add the tomatoes, tomato purée, kidney beans, cinnamon, wine and seasoning. Bring to the boil then simmer for 10 minutes.

3 In a medium-size saucepan, mix the cornflour with a little of the milk to make a paste. Beat in the remaining milk then cook over a moderate heat, stirring frequently, until thickened. Mix in half the cheese, season to taste then remove the pan from the heat. Allow the sauce to cool slightly then beat in the egg.

4 Arrange half of the baked aubergine slices in the base of a shallow, ovenproof dish. Spoon over half of the bean mixture then half of the white sauce. Repeat the layers, finishing with the white sauce. Scatter the remaining cheese over.

5 Bake for about 1 hour, until golden and bubbling.

TOP TIPS This dish tastes even better when warmed up the following day, as the flavours have had time to develop.

Use low-fat cooking spray instead of olive oil and save 1 point per serving.

Rich bean moussaka: Delicious with a slice of warm fresh bread for only 7 points per serving!

Italian stuffed pancakes: Heavenly.

ITALIAN STUFFED PANCAKES

POINTS

per recipe: 30   per serving: 7½

Ⓥ *Serves 4*
Preparation time: 50 minutes
Cooking time: 30 minutes
Calories per serving: 435
Freezing: recommended

This dish was recommended by Jane Prescott, an Area Service Manager. The pancakes are delicious served with an assortment of steamed vegetables or a crisp green salad.

FOR THE PANCAKES

110 g (4 oz) plain white flour
a pinch of salt
1 egg
300 ml (½ pint) skimmed milk
2 teaspoons vegetable oil

FOR THE FILLING

1 teaspoon vegetable oil
1 onion, chopped
2 garlic cloves, crushed
1 small leek, chopped
225 g (8 oz) frozen spinach, defrosted and squeezed
225 g (8 oz) potatoes, boiled and diced
225 g (8 oz) ricotta cheese
a pinch of freshly ground nutmeg
salt and freshly ground black pepper

FOR THE TOPPING

1 tablespoon olive oil
1 small onion, chopped
400 g (14 oz) canned chopped tomatoes with herbs
25 g (1 oz) Cheddar cheese, grated

1 To make the pancakes, sift the flour and salt into a bowl then make a well in the centre. Break the egg into the well then beat it in with a wooden spoon. Gradually beat in the milk, drawing the flour in from the sides, to make a smooth batter.

2 Heat an 18 cm (7-inch) non-stick frying pan. Dip a piece of kitchen paper in the oil and wipe it around the pan to grease it lightly. Pour just enough batter to coat the base of the pan thinly. Cook for 1–2 minutes, until the pancake is golden. Turn or toss the pancake over and cook the second side until golden. Transfer it to a plate then repeat the process with the remaining batter, greasing the pan each time, to make eight pancakes. Stack them, interleaved with baking parchment as you go.

3 Preheat the oven to Gas Mark 6/ 200°C/fan oven 180°C.

4 To make the filling, heat the oil in a medium-size frying pan then gently cook the onion, garlic and leek, until softened. Stir in the spinach and cook for 1 more minute. Remove the pan from the heat then stir in the potatoes, ricotta cheese and nutmeg. Season to taste.

5 To make the topping, heat the oil in a small pan then sauté the onion until soft. Add the tomatoes with herbs and cook for another 5 minutes. If you want a smooth sauce, put the mixture in a blender and blend until smooth.

6 Divide the filling equally between the pancakes – spooning it across one end. Roll up the pancakes then arrange them, with the opening underneath, in a shallow, ovenproof dish. Pour the topping over then sprinkle with the Cheddar cheese.

7 Bake the pancakes for 30 minutes, or until the topping bubbles. Serve immediately.

TOP TIP The pancake batter ingredients can be mixed together in a food processor or blender. Put the egg and liquid in first then add the flour and process until smooth.

MUSHROOM AND PEPPER CHILLI

POINTS

per recipe: 18½   **per serving:** 4½

ⓥ *Serves 4*
Preparation time: 35 minutes
Cooking time: 20–30 minutes
Calories per serving: 320
Freezing: recommended

This recipe was also recommended by Jane Prescott, and was first published in 1994. Here the chilli is served with salad and taco chips, but you can serve with rice or as a filling for a jacket potato, remembering to adjust the points accordingly.

FOR THE CHILLI

1 tablespoon vegetable oil

1 large onion, chopped

1 garlic clove, chopped

1 fresh red chilli pepper, de-seeded and chopped finely or 2 teaspoons chilli powder

1 large red or green pepper, de-seeded and chopped

250 g (9 oz) mushrooms, sliced

400 g can chopped tomatoes

2 tablespoons tomato purée

400 g (14 oz) canned red kidney beans, rinsed and drained

300 ml (½ pint) vegetable stock

1 teaspoon dried mixed herbs

2 tablespoons cornflour

salt and freshly ground black pepper

FOR THE SALAD

60 g (2 oz) Iceburg lettuce, shredded

2 tomatoes, quartered

5 cm (2-inch) piece of cucumber, sliced

1 teaspoon olive oil

1 tablespoon lemon juice or cider vinegar

salt and freshly ground pepper

TO SERVE

90 g (3¼ oz) taco chips

1 Heat the vegetable oil in large saucepan. Sauté the onion, garlic, fresh chilli or chilli powder and red or green pepper for 3–4 minutes, until softened. Add the mushrooms and cook for 2 minutes more.

2 Pour in the tomatoes and stir in the tomato purée. Add the kidney beans, stock and herbs then bring to the boil. Reduce the heat then simmer, covered, for 20–30 minutes.

3 Blend the cornflour with a little water and mix it into the saucepan. Cook, stirring, for 2 minutes or until thickened. Taste and check the seasoning.

4 In a salad bowl, toss together the lettuce, tomatoes, cucumber, olive oil and lemon juice or vinegar. Season with salt and pepper.

5 Serve the chilli in warmed bowls, accompanied by the salad and the taco chips.

TOP TIP Use low-fat cooking spray instead of vegetable oil in the chilli to save ½ a point per serving.

CREAMY BAKED VEGETABLES

POINTS

per recipe: 21   **per serving:** 5½

ⓥ *Serves 4*
Preparation time: 20 minutes
Cooking time: 20 minutes
Calories per serving: 350
Freezing: not recommended

This warming and hearty dish, published in 1995, was recommended for the anniversary cookbook by Louise Iles. It is wonderful served with assorted zero point steamed vegetables.

250 g (9 oz) parsnips, peeled and cut into 5 cm (2-inch) sticks

250 g (9 oz) swede, peeled and cut into 5 cm (2-inch) sticks

225 g (8 oz) potatoes, peeled and cut into 5 cm (2-inch) sticks

350 g (12 oz) low-fat plain fromage frais

2 eggs, beaten

60 g (2 oz) Cheddar cheese, grated

salt and freshly ground black pepper

1 Preheat the oven to Gas Mark 6/ 200°C/fan oven 180°C.

2 Blanch all the vegetables in boiling water for 2–3 minutes or until tender to the bite. Drain them well then transfer to an ovenproof dish.

3 Whisk the fromage frais, eggs and seasoning together then spoon this mixture over the vegetables. Sprinkle the Cheddar cheese over and bake for 20 minutes, until golden and bubbling.

Mixed mushroom pasta: Comforting and delicious.

MIXED MUSHROOM PASTA

POINTS

per recipe: 33   per serving: 8½

Ⓥ Serves 4

Preparation time: 40 minutes
Cooking time: 20 minutes
Calories per serving: 575
Freezing: not recommended

This recipe, first published in 1995, is ideal for when you are in a hurry and have hungry mouths to feed. Serve it with a crisp zero point salad.

250 g (9 oz) pasta
2 tablespoons olive oil
2 garlic cloves, chopped
110 g (4 oz) baby button mushrooms
175 g (6 oz) chestnut mushrooms, quartered
175 g (6 oz) small open-cup mushrooms, sliced
1 teaspoon dried rosemary
2 tablespoons plain white flour
150 ml (¼ pint) skimmed milk
350 g (12 oz) low-fat plain fromage frais
60 g (2 oz) Cheddar cheese, grated
salt and freshly ground black pepper
fresh parsley, chopped, to serve

1 Preheat the oven to Gas Mark 5/ 190°C/fan oven 170°C.

2 Cook the pasta in lightly salted boiling water for 10 minutes or according to packet instructions. Drain well.

3 Meanwhile, heat the oil in a large frying pan then fry the garlic, mushrooms and rosemary for 10 minutes over a low heat. Season to taste.

4 Stir in the flour and cook for 1 minute. Gradually add in the milk, stirring continuously, until thickened.

5 Remove the pan from the heat and transfer the mixture to a large ovenproof dish. Stir in the drained pasta, fromage frais and seasoning.

6 Sprinkle the Cheddar cheese over then bake for 20 minutes or until bubbling. Serve immediately, garnished with a sprinkling of parsley.

TOP TIP Use low-fat cooking spray instead of olive oil to save 1½ points per serving.

SHEPHERDESS PIE

POINTS

per recipe: 22   per serving: 5½

Ⓥ Serves 4

Preparation time: 15–20 minutes
Cooking time: 1 hour 10 minutes
Calories per serving: 385
Freezing: recommended

This dish, which Janet Carney put forward, was originally published in 1997. Janet says that she often shuts herself away in her kitchen on a Sunday to cook this recipe, and then freezes it in separate portions to keep her going for the week ahead!

2 teaspoons sunflower oil
1 leek, chopped finely
1 small courgette, diced
1 carrot, diced
1 garlic clove, crushed
110 g (4 oz) mushrooms, sliced
60 g (2 oz) dried red lentils
60 g (2 oz) dried green lentils
225 g (8 oz) canned chopped tomatoes
1 bay leaf
½ teaspoon dried marjoram
½ teaspoon dried thyme
1½ tablespoons brown sauce
220 g (7½ oz) canned baked beans
salt and freshly ground black pepper

FOR THE TOPPING

900 g (2 lb) potatoes, peeled
5–6 tablespoons skimmed milk
25 g (1 oz) half-fat Cheddar cheese, grated
salt and freshly ground black pepper

1 Preheat the oven to Gas Mark 6/ 200°C/fan oven 180°C.

2 Heat the oil in a large saucepan then gently fry the leek, courgette, carrot, garlic and mushrooms for 10 minutes.

3 Add the lentils, tomatoes, 450 ml (16 fl oz) water, the bay leaf and the herbs. Bring the mixture to the boil then reduce the heat. Partially cover the pan and simmer for 30 minutes or until the lentils are soft and the mixture is thick. Stir in the brown sauce and baked beans then cook for a further 5 minutes.

4 Meanwhile, make the topping. Place the potatoes in a pan of salted water, bring to the boil then simmer for about 20 minutes, until tender. Drain the potatoes, return them to the pan then heat gently to dry them out. Mash the potatoes with the milk and seasoning.

5 Remove the bay leaf from the lentil mixture and check the seasoning. Spoon the mixture into a large, ovenproof dish. Pile the mash on top and fork it over. Sprinkle with the grated cheese.

6 Bake in the oven for 15–20 minutes or until the potato is crispy. Serve immediately.

PASTA PRIMAVERA

POINTS

per recipe: 22   per serving: 5½

V Serves 4

Preparation and cooking time: 30 minutes

Calories per serving: 375

Freezing: not recommended

This wonderfully colourful recipe was first written in 1986 and was proposed by Berendina Williams, a Diamond Leader from Leicestershire. Berendina says it looks great so it's super as a party piece.

240 g (8½ oz) fettuccine

300 g (10½ oz) Quark

125 ml (4 fl oz) skimmed milk

low-fat cooking spray

3–4 garlic cloves, chopped finely

1 red pepper, de-seeded and cut into matchsticks

110 g (4 oz) asparagus, cooked and cut into diagonal, bite-size pieces

110 g (4 oz) carrots, sliced and cooked

60 g (2 oz) Parmesan cheese, grated

salt and freshly ground black pepper

1 Bring a large pan of salted water to the boil. Add the pasta and cook for 6–8 minutes, until al dente.

2 Meanwhile, place the Quark and milk in a blender or food processor then process until smooth. Set aside.

3 Heat a large pan and spray with low-fat cooking spray. Sauté the garlic briefly – do not let it brown. Pour the Quark mixture into the pan and bring it to the boil.

4 Drain the pasta and add it, together with all the remaining ingredients including the Parmesan, to the Quark mixture. Season well. Toss all the ingredients to coat the vegetables and pasta with the sauce. Serve as soon as the vegetables have heated through.

RED LENTIL AND VEGETABLE CURRY

POINTS

per recipe: 14   per serving: 3½

V Serves 4

Preparation time: 20 minutes

Cooking time: 25 minutes

Calories per serving: 320

Freezing: not recommended

This great recipe was published in 1993 and has been recommended by Louise Iles. It is a wonderful alternative to all those high-point take-away curries.

1½ tablespoons sunflower oil

1 large onion, chopped finely

2 garlic cloves, chopped finely

175 g (6 oz) carrots, diced

2 sticks celery, diced

4 tablespoons curry powder

400 g can chopped tomatoes

225 g (8 oz) dried red lentils

600 ml (1 pint) vegetable stock

lemon juice

salt and freshly ground black pepper

1 Heat the oil in a large saucepan then stir-fry the onion and garlic for 3 minutes. Add the carrots and celery, stir, then add the curry powder.

2 Stir in the tomatoes, lentils and stock and bring to the boil over a moderate heat. Cover the saucepan, reduce the heat and simmer for 20–25 minutes, stirring occasionally. If necessary add a little more stock.

3 Season to taste with lemon juice, salt and pepper then serve.

TOP TIP Try experimenting with different zero point vegetables, or adding more. Cauliflower and swede have a good texture for absorbing all the delicious curry flavours. Use a mild or hot curry powder according to your taste.

Red lentil and vegetable curry: Only 7½ points per serving for curry with half a medium naan bread!

Winter vegetable
casserole with
spicy dumplings:
Something special
for only 5½ points
per serving.

WINTER VEGETABLE CASSEROLE WITH SPICY DUMPLINGS

POINTS

per recipe: 21   per serving: 5½

ⓥ Serves 4

Preparation time: 30 minutes
Cooking time: 40 minutes
Calories per serving: 335
Freezing: recommended

First published in 1994, this recipe is great for warming you up on those cold winter days. Try exchanging some of the zero point vegetables for your own zero point favourites, to give it that personal touch.

FOR THE DUMPLINGS

90 g (3¼ oz) self-raising white flour
a pinch of salt
1 teaspoon ground coriander
1 teaspoon cumin seeds
2 tablespoons polyunsaturated margarine

FOR THE CASSEROLE

2 teaspoons vegetable oil
90 g (3¼ oz) shallots or small onions, halved
1 leek, sliced
1 large carrot, sliced
225 g (8 oz) parsnips, chopped
2 celery sticks, chopped
1.2 litres (2 pints) vegetable stock
25 g (1 oz) pearl barley or bulghar wheat
400 g (14 oz) canned chick-peas, rinsed and drained
175 g (6 oz) cauliflower, broken into florets
salt and freshly ground black pepper
a handful of parsley or coriander, to garnish (optional)

1 Sift the flour and salt into a large bowl then mix in the ground coriander and cumin seeds. Rub in the margarine until the mixture resembles fine breadcrumbs. Add enough cold water to make a soft, but not sticky, dough. Form into eight dumplings, cover then set aside.

2 Heat the oil in a large saucepan then sauté the shallots or onions, leek, carrot, parsnips and celery for 5 minutes, without browning them.

3 Add the stock, pearl barley or bulghar wheat, and chick-peas to the saucepan. Bring to the boil then reduce the heat, cover, and simmer for 20 minutes.

4 Add the cauliflower and dumplings to the saucepan. Cover and simmer for 20 minutes or until the dumplings are cooked – they should be light and fluffy.

5 Season the casserole to taste. Serve, garnished with parsley or coriander if desired, allowing two dumplings per person.

PARSNIP-TOPPED PIE

POINTS

per recipe: 10   per serving: 5

ⓥ Serves 2

Preparation and cooking time: 55 minutes
Calories per serving: 285
Freezing: not recommended

This dish is a popular recipe, and was published in 1990. Using parsnip as a pie topping makes a tasty variation to mashed potato and this recipe makes a great filling meal for those hungry days.

1 teaspoon vegetable oil
½ onion, chopped
¼ teaspoon oregano
½ teaspoon chilli sauce
225 g (8 oz) canned chopped tomatoes
220 g (7½ oz) freshly cooked or canned kidney beans, rinsed and drained
400 g (14 oz) parsnips, cut into chunks
2 tablespoons skimmed milk
25 g (1 oz) half-fat mature Cheddar cheese, grated
salt and freshly ground black pepper

1 Heat the oil in a medium-size saucepan. Add the onion and stir-fry for 3–4 minutes.

2 Stir the oregano, chilli sauce and tomatoes into the saucepan. Bring to the boil then partially cover. Reduce the heat and simmer for 10 minutes.

3 Stir in the kidney beans then season. Partially cover the saucepan and simmer for about 10 minutes, until the sauce is fairly thick.

4 Meanwhile, cook the parsnips for 12–13 minutes in boiling salted water, until tender, then drain.

5 Mash the parsnips until smooth, then stir in the milk.

6 Spoon the beans and tomatoes into a small, flameproof dish then top with the parsnip mash. Sprinkle the cheese over.

7 Place under a preheated hot grill for 2–3 minutes, until golden.

TOP TIPS The base of this pie can be made in advance and frozen, if desired. When required, just defrost, then heat it through. Top it with the parsnip mixture then grill.

Use low-fat cooking spray instead of vegetable oil and save ½ a point per serving.

desserts
& puddings

The naughtiest of puddings, without the points! Tuck into your favourite desserts: Tiramisu (page 50), Lemon Cheesecake (page 46) or Baby Bread and Butter Puds (page 45), without worry. If you're entertaining then this chapter will ensure that you can serve a luscious dessert or pudding, and your guests will never know it's a low-fat version. And if you're on your own and need a sweetener, then try Light Date and Banana Pudding (page 50), a recipe just for one.

CHOCOLATE APRICOT CHEESECAKE

POINTS

per recipe: 52   per slice: 4½

Makes 12 slices
Preparation time: 40 minutes +
2-3 hours chilling
Calories per slice: 250
Freezing: not recommended

Sue Hughes, a Leader from Derby, put forward this recipe for the 35 year anniversary cookbook. As a self-confessed chocoholic, Sue finds this dish 'a wonderfully tasty treat'.

40 g (1½ oz) dark chocolate
90 g (3¼ oz) polyunsaturated margarine
2 teaspoons cocoa powder
12 large digestive biscuits
300 g (10½ oz) curd cheese
175 g (6 oz) low-fat plain fromage frais
300 g (10½ oz) canned apricots, drained, reserving 6 tablespoons of juice
2 tablespoons fresh orange juice
1½ tablespoons sugar
1 sachet gelatine
2 egg whites
pinch of cream of tartar

1 Break half the chocolate into a cup then stand it in a saucepan of simmering water until it melts. Melt the margarine in a small saucepan, then take it off the heat.

2 Stir the cocoa powder into the melted margarine, add the melted chocolate and stir well. Break the remaining chocolate into the cup and set aside.

3 Crush the biscuits to make crumbs then stir them into the margarine and chocolate. Spoon the crumb mixture into a 20 cm (8-inch) spring-form tin and spread it firmly over the base.

4 Put the curd cheese, fromage frais, apricots, half the reserved juice, orange juice and sugar into a food processor. Process to make a purée.

5 Pour the remaining reserved juice into a cup then sprinkle in the gelatine. Stir then stand the cup in a saucepan of simmering water until the gelatine dissolves.

6 Add the dissolved gelatine to the purée in the food processor. Blend once again then pour it into a bowl and chill.

7 Whisk the egg whites together with the cream of tartar into soft peaks. Gently fold them into the chilled purée then pour this mixture into the tin.

8 Grate the remaining chocolate into a cup and stand it in a saucepan of simmering water until it melts. Using a fork, drizzle the melted chocolate over the top of the cheesecake then swirl to make an attractive design. Chill until completely set.

9 To serve, remove the side of the tin then slide the cheesecake onto a flat serving plate.

Chocolate apricot cheesecake: Each gorgeous slice is only 4½ points.

Baby bread and
butter puds:
Only 4½ points
each!

BABY BREAD AND BUTTER PUDS

POINTS

per recipe: $17\frac{1}{2}$	per serving: $4\frac{1}{2}$

Ⓥ *Serves 4*
Preparation time: 25 minutes + 30 minutes standing
Cooking time: 20–30 minutes
Calories per serving: 260
Freezing: not recommended

The recipe for these delightful, individual puddings was originally written in 1999. They were suggested to us for the anniversary cookbook by Janet Carney, who thinks they are wonderful – and we have to agree!

1 tablespoon mixed peel (optional)
50 g (1¾ oz) sultanas or raisins
grated zest of 1 lemon or small orange

6 medium slices of white bread, crusts removed
4 teaspoons low-fat spread
low-fat cooking spray
350 ml (12 fl oz) skimmed milk
3 tablespoons unrefined soft brown sugar
2 eggs

1 Mix the peel, if using, with the sultanas or raisins and the grated zest.

2 Using pastry cutters, cut twelve discs out of the bread to fit inside four medium-size ramekins. Spread the bread lightly with the low-fat spread.

3 Spray the insides of the ramekins with cooking spray then place a bread disc in the bottom of each one. Divide half the fruit mixture evenly between the ramekins. Repeat the layer of bread and fruit, and top with a bread disc – the low-fat spread side should face up.

4 In a small saucepan, bring the milk to the boil with the soft brown sugar, stirring until the sugar has dissolved. Remove the pan from the heat and set aside to cool for 5 minutes.

5 Meanwhile, beat the eggs in a large, heatproof bowl. Add the milk mixture to the eggs and beat well. Slowly pour the mixture over each filled ramekin, making sure it seeps inside.

6 Leave the ramekins for about 30 minutes to allow the bread to absorb the liquid. Meanwhile, preheat the oven to Gas Mark 5/ 190°C/fan oven 170°C.

7 Stand the ramekins in a small roasting pan. Pour hot water into the pan so it comes two-thirds of the way up the dishes. Bake for 20–30 minutes or until risen, golden and crisp on top. Allow them to stand for 5 minutes before serving.

YOGURT FRUIT PIE

POINTS

per recipe: $34\frac{1}{2}$	per serving: $4\frac{1}{2}$

Serves 8
Preparation and cooking time: 25 minutes + cooling + 4 hours chilling
Calories per serving: 245
Freezing: not recommended

This recipe was recommended by Lynne Senior, a Leader from Aberdeenshire. It comes from the first Weight Watchers cookbook she ever bought, which was published in 1986!

FOR THE CRUST
16 digestive biscuits, crushed
8 teaspoons polyunsaturated margarine, melted

FOR THE FILLING
4 tablespoons fresh orange juice
8 teaspoons sugar
1 sachet gelatine
450 ml (16 fl oz) low-fat plain yogurt
110 g (4 oz) canned crushed pineapple, no sugar added
1 teaspoon vanilla essence

FOR THE TOPPING
90 g (3¼ oz) small seedless black grapes
90 g (3¼ oz) small seedless green grapes
150 g (5½ oz) strawberries, halved

1 Preheat the oven to Gas Mark 4/ 180°C/fan oven 160°C. Thoroughly mix the biscuits and margarine together. Using the back of a spoon, press the crumb mixture over the base and sides of a 23 cm (9-inch) flan dish. Bake for 10 minutes or until the pie crust is crisp and brown. Leave to cool.

2 Pour the orange juice into a small cup then sprinkle in the sugar and gelatine. Stand the cup in a pan of simmering water and stir until the gelatine and sugar has dissolved. Set aside.

3 Gently mix the yogurt and pineapple together then stir in the gelatine mixture and vanilla essence. Pour the mixture into the piecrust. Cover and refrigerate for 4 hours, or until firm. Use within 8 hours.

4 To serve, arrange the fruit topping decoratively over the pie then serve immediately.

VARIATION For a delicious alternative, replace the pineapple filling with 110 g (4 oz) of mashed banana and substitute the grapes with orange segments. The points per serving will remain the same.

LEMON CHEESECAKE

POINTS

per recipe: 24	per slice: 2½

Makes 10 slices
Preparation and cooking time: 1 hour
+ 1½ hours setting + 2-3 hours
chilling
Calories per slice: 135
Freezing: not recommended

Louise Iles highlighted this recipe as one of her favourites.

1 egg plus 3 egg whites
60 g (2 oz) caster sugar
40 g (1½ oz) plain white flour
15 g (½ oz) cornflour
½ teaspoon baking powder
250 g (9 oz) low-fat cottage cheese
250 g (9 oz) curd cheese
350 ml (12 fl oz) skimmed milk
¼ teaspoon vanilla essence
1½ tablespoons lemon juice
artificial sweetener
1 sachet of gelatine
a pinch of cream of tartar

1 Preheat the oven to Gas Mark 4/ 180°C/fan oven 160°C. Line the base and sides of a 25 cm (10-inch) loose-bottomed flan tin with non-stick baking parchment.

2 Break the whole egg into a medium-size bowl, add the caster sugar then place the bowl on top of a saucepan of simmering water. Whisk continuously until thick and creamy, so that when the whisk is lifted it leaves a trail.

3 Sift the flour, cornflour and baking powder together then gently fold into the whisked mixture together with 1 tablespoon of warm water. Spoon the mixture evenly over the base of the lined flan tin so that hardly any spreading is required. Bake for about 15 minutes or until golden – when lightly pressed the cake should feel springy. Leave to cool in the flan tin. When cold turn out the sponge on a plate then remove the paper base.

4 Re-line the flan tin and sides with baking parchment, securing the paper so that it is about 4 cm (1½ inches) higher than the sides of the tin. Place the sponge back in the tin.

5 Process the cottage cheese and curd cheese with the milk in a liquidiser or food processor until smooth. Add the vanilla essence and lemon juice then process once again. Pour into a bowl. Sweeten to taste with artificial sweetener.

6 Put 2 tablespoons of cold water in a cup or small bowl. Sprinkle the gelatine in then stand the cup in a saucepan of simmering water until the gelatine has dissolved. Stir a little of the cheese and milk mixture into the gelatine then pour this back into the cheese mixture. Leave for 1–1½ hours, until thick and beginning to set.

7 Whisk the egg whites together with the cream of tartar until they form peaks. Using a metal spoon, fold the whisked egg whites into the setting mixture. Spoon the cheese mixture on top of the sponge base then chill until completely set. To serve, transfer the cheesecake to a flat serving plate then slide off the paper.

STRAWBERRY PUFFS

POINTS

per recipe: 14	per serving: 3½

Serves 4
Preparation time: 20 minutes + cooling
Cooking time: 20 minutes
Calories per serving: 175
Freezing: not recommended

Lynda Warlow, an Area Service Manager from Kent, recommended this recipe as a great dinner party dessert.

40 g (1½ oz) plain white flour
a pinch of salt
2 tablespoons polyunsaturated margarine
1 egg, beaten
200 ml (7 fl oz) very low-fat strawberry fromage frais
175 g (6 oz) strawberries, chopped
2 tablespoons icing sugar
1-2 drops of red food colouring

1 Preheat the oven to Gas Mark 7/ 220°C/fan oven 200°C. Sift the flour and salt together on to a plate.

2 In a small saucepan gently melt the margarine with 5 tablespoons of water. Bring to the boil, remove from the heat then quickly add the flour all at once. Beat until the mixture forms a soft ball and leaves the side of the pan clean. Cool slightly.

3 Gradually beat in the egg until the mixture is thick and glossy. Dampen a baking sheet. Place 12 heaped teaspoonfuls of the mixture on to the baking sheet. Bake in the oven for 15–20 minutes, until well risen and golden. Split the puffs at once so that the steam escapes. Leave to cool.

4 Just before serving, mix together the fromage frais and most of the strawberries. Use this to fill the puffs. Divide between four plates. Top with the remaining strawberries.

5 Blend the icing sugar with a little water to make a thin glacé icing. Add 1–2 drops of red food colouring to give a pretty pink colour then drizzle over the top of the strawberry puffs.

Strawberry puffs:
Enjoy three for
only 3½ points!

Drop scones with ice cream and butterscotch sauce: All this for only 4 points.

DROP SCONES WITH ICE CREAM AND BUTTERSCOTCH SAUCE

POINTS

per recipe: 15	per serving: 4

Ⓥ *Serves 4*

Preparation and cooking time: 30 minutes

Calories per serving: 245

Freezing: not recommended

This recipe was suggested by Christine Younger who became a Leader in 1986, after losing an amazing 68½ lbs to get to her Goal. Christine says that 'it's a gorgeous pudding, leaving you scraping the plate for more!'

FOR THE BATTER

110 g (4 oz) plain white flour

½ teaspoon baking powder

a pinch of salt

1 egg, beaten

200 ml (7 fl oz) skimmed milk

low-fat cooking spray

FOR THE SAUCE

1 tablespoon polyunsaturated margarine

2 tablespoons golden syrup

2 tablespoons caster sugar

1 teaspoon lemon juice

TO SERVE

110 g (4 oz) vanilla low-fat ice cream

1 Put the flour, baking powder, salt, egg and milk into a large bowl then whisk together until smooth.

2 Heat a heavy-based frying pan and spray once with the low-fat cooking spray. Add tablespoons of batter to the pan to make drop scones. You should be able to fit 4–5 tablespoons of batter in the pan. Cook gently, turning them over as bubbles begin to appear on the surface. Cook the other side for about 1 minute more. Transfer to sheets of greaseproof paper once cooked, and keep them covered, in a warm place. Cook the remaining batter in the same way, making about 20 scones.

3 To make the sauce, gently heat the margarine, syrup, sugar and lemon juice together until dissolved, stirring constantly. Do not allow the mixture to boil. Serve five drop scones each, with the hot sauce and ice cream.

VARIATION Serve the scones with chopped bananas and maple syrup, instead of the sauce. But remember to alter the points accordingly.

APRICOT AND BANANA MERINGUE

POINTS

per recipe: 8	per serving: 2

Ⓥ *Serves 4*

Preparation and cooking time: 35 minutes + cooling

Calories per serving: 140

Freezing: not recommended

Jane Prescott, an Area Service Manager from Lincoln, highlighted this scrumptious dessert as one of her favourites. It's easy to prepare, tastes delicious and yet is so low in points.

450 g (1 lb) fresh apricots, halved and stoned

1 tablespoon cornflour, blended with a little water

artificial sweetener, to taste

1 banana

2 eggs, separated

1 tablespoon caster sugar

1 Preheat the oven to Gas Mark 4/ 180°C/fan oven 160°C.

2 Simmer the apricots in 200 ml (7 fl oz) of water for about 10 minutes, until soft and pulpy. Remove from the heat, stir in the blended cornflour then cook gently for about 2 minutes, until the mixture has thickened. Add artificial sweetener to taste. Cool slightly.

3 Slice the banana and stir it into the apricots with the egg yolks. Transfer the mixture to an ovenproof dish.

4 Whisk the egg whites until stiff. Add the caster sugar, then whisk again until stiff and glossy. Pile the whipped egg whites on top of the fruit mixture then bake for approximately 10 minutes, until the meringue is golden.

5 Divide between four plates and serve warm.

Apricot and banana meringue: Only 2 points per serving.

**Tiramisu:
Only 3½ points.**

TIRAMISU

POINTS

per recipe: 13   **per serving: 3½**

Serves 4
Preparation time: 20 minutes + 30
minutes chilling
Calories per serving: 175
Freezing: not recommended

Written in 1999 this recipe was
recommended by Linda Clifton,
a Diamond Leader, who says,
'This tiramisu is to die for!'

250 g (9 oz) Quark
4 tablespoons low-fat plain yogurt
1 tablespoon caster sugar
½ teaspoon vanilla essence
125 ml (4 fl oz) strong black coffee
2 tablespoons Tia Maria or Kahlua
(optional)
16 sponge fingers (boudoir biscuits),
halved
1 teaspoon cocoa powder, for sprinkling

1 In a medium-size bowl, beat
together the Quark, yogurt, caster
sugar and vanilla essence to make
a smooth cream.
2 In a separate bowl, mix together
the coffee and Tia Maria or Kahlua,
if using.
3 Dip the sponge fingers in the
coffee mixture, one at a time. Leave
them to soak for 10–20 seconds, so
that they absorb some of the mixture
without becoming too soggy.
4 Place the fingers around the inside
of four glass serving bowls. Spoon in
the yogurt mixture.
5 Chill in the refrigerator for at least
30 minutes then sprinkle with the
cocoa powder and serve.

TOP TIP If you aren't using alcohol,
you'll need extra tablespoons of
strong black coffee.

LIGHT DATE AND BANANA PUDDING

POINTS

per recipe: 4   **per serving: 4**

v Serves 1
Preparation and cooking time: 30
minutes
Calories per serving: 295
Freezing: not recommended

This delicious dessert is great for
when you're on your own and crave
something sweet. So go on – treat
yourself!

1 banana
a few drops of lemon juice
1 egg, separated
1 tablespoon skimmed milk
15 g (½ oz) dates, chopped
a pinch of ground nutmeg
2 teaspoons caster sugar

1 Preheat the oven to Gas Mark 5/
190°C/fan oven 170°C.
2 In a medium-size bowl, mash the
banana with the lemon juice then
mix in the egg yolk, milk, dates and
nutmeg. Transfer the mixture to a
small, ovenproof dish then bake for
10–15 minutes, until lightly set.
3 Beat the egg white until stiff then
whisk in the sugar to form a stiff,
glossy meringue mixture. Pile this on
top of the banana base then cook for
5 more minutes, until golden. Serve
at once.

CRISPY GINGER BASKETS

V *Serves 6*

Preparation and cooking time: 30 minutes + cooling
Calories per basket: 190
Freezing: not recommended

This recipe for fruit-filled baskets was first published in 1991 and is great for all the family. Fill the baskets only a short while before serving, otherwise the biscuit will begin to soften.

2 tablespoons golden syrup
25 g (1 oz) soft brown sugar
25 g (1 oz) polyunsaturated margarine
25 g (1 oz) plain flour
$^{1}/_{2}$ teaspoon ground ginger
1 banana
110 g (4 oz) low-fat, plain fromage frais
$^{1}/_{4}$ – $^{1}/_{2}$ teaspoon lemon juice
2 mangoes
2 kiwi fruit

1 Place the syrup, sugar and margarine in a bowl. Sieve the flour and ginger into a separate bowl then set aside.

2 Place the bowl containing the syrup mixture in the microwave then cook on Medium for 1 minute 40 seconds. Stir well then add the flour and ginger and mix until evenly blended.

3 Lay a 15 cm (6-inch) circle of non-stick baking parchment on the microwave turntable. Spoon about one-sixth of the syrup mixture onto the centre of the paper then cook on High for about 1 minute, until the mixture has spread and is a bubbling, dark golden colour. Slide the paper carefully off the turntable then continue cooking the remaining mixture in the same way.

4 Allow each biscuit to cool on the paper for 1–2 minutes then gently lift the edges of the circle and transfer to an upturned small basin or round-bottomed cup. Lay the biscuit over the base of the bowl or cup and very gently and lightly press the edge down. Leave until completely cold.

5 Just before serving, mash the banana together with the fromage frais, adding a little lemon juice to taste. Halve, then dice the mangoes. Slice the kiwi fruit, then cut each slice in two or three pieces.

6 Spoon the fromage frais mixture into each ginger biscuit basket then arrange the mango and kiwi on top.

VARIATION For that extra-special occasion, drizzle the top with melted chocolate – but don't forget to add on the extra points.

Crispy ginger baskets: Fantastic flavours for only $2^{1}/_{2}$ points each.

cakes
& bakes

Nothing beats the smell or taste of home-baked cakes and biscuits. Even if you have not done much baking before you won't find any of these recipes difficult, and once you have baked your own cakes you will never crave the shop bought variety again! This chapter gives a huge variety of easy to follow recipes including Flapjacks (page 59), Double Chocolate Cookies (page 59) and even Sticky Cinnamon Buns (page 63), to help you through those sweet-craving moments. Don't deprive yourself of these wonderful sweet, low-point treats.

CRUMBLY APPLE CAKE

POINTS

per recipe: 42   per slice: 2½

V Makes 16 slices
Preparation time: 20 minutes + cooling
Cooking time: 50–55 minutes
Calories per slice: 160
Freezing: recommended

A wonderful recipe that was recommended by Jackie Cowie, Sylvia Palmer, Anja Leeves and Helen Perry. Helen says it's 'mouth-watering', Sylvia declares it 'wonderful', Anja says it's her favourite cake and Jackie says it's great with custard!

110 g (4 oz) polyunsaturated margarine
110 g (4 oz) soft brown sugar
110 g (4 oz) self-raising white flour
110 g (4 oz) self-raising wholemeal flour
a pinch of salt
1 egg, beaten
450 g (1 lb) cooking apples, peeled, cored and sliced
110 g (4 oz) sultanas
½ teaspoon ground cinnamon
25 g (1 oz) demerara sugar

1 Preheat the oven to Gas Mark 5/ 190°C/fan oven 170°C. Grease a 20 cm (8-inch) cake tin with ½ a teaspoon of the margarine then line it with non-stick baking parchment.

2 Melt the remaining margarine in a small saucepan then, in a large bowl, mix it with the soft brown sugar, flours, salt and beaten egg to make a stiff dough. Put about two-thirds of this dough in the prepared tin and press down.

3 In a clean bowl, mix together the apples, sultanas, cinnamon and demerara sugar. Spread the mixture in an even layer over the dough in the tin. Top with the remaining dough – the surface will be uneven.

4 Bake the cake for 50–55 minutes. Cool in the tin for 10 minutes then remove it and place on a cooling rack. Allow it to cool completely, before cutting it into 16 slices.

Crumbly apple cake: Unbelievably low in points.

Plaited cheese and herb scone: Take a break and enjoy a slice with a cup of tea!

PLAITED CHEESE AND HERB SCONE

POINTS

| per recipe: 35 | per scone: $4^{1/2}$ |

V *Serves 8*
Preparation time: 25 minutes
Cooking time: 15 minutes
Calories per scone: 225
Freezing: recommended

This savoury snack hits the spot.

60 g (2 oz) polyunsaturated margarine
250 g (9 oz) self-raising white flour
a pinch of salt
110 g (4 oz) Lancashire or Cheshire cheese, grated
1 tablespoon chopped fresh mixed herbs or 1½ teaspoons dried herbs
1 egg
150 ml (¼ pint) skimmed milk

1 Preheat the oven to Gas Mark 7/ 220°C/fan oven 200°C. Grease a baking sheet with ½ a teaspoon of the margarine.
2 Sift the flour and salt into a large mixing bowl. Rub in the remaining margarine until the mixture resembles fine breadcrumbs. Stir in half the cheese and all the herbs.
3 Beat the egg and milk together. Gradually add to the flour mixture until it forms a soft dough. Knead until smooth.
4 Turn the dough on to a lightly floured surface and divide it into three equal pieces. Roll each piece into a sausage shape then plait together, pressing the ends together to seal them.
5 Place the plait on the baking sheet and brush it with any remaining egg and milk mixture. Sprinkle with the remaining cheese.
6 Bake for 12–15 minutes or until well risen and golden. Serve hot.

MALT LOAF

POINTS

| per recipe: 18 | per slice: $1^{1/2}$ |

V *Makes 12 slices*
Preparation time: 15 minutes + cooling + 1 day resting
Calories per slice: 110
Freezing: recommended

Sally Debenham, a Leader from Woodbridge, recommended this recipe. Sally often cooks it then cuts the loaf into slices and puts them in the freezer, ready to take out when friends come round.

225 g (8 oz) self-raising white flour
25 g (1 oz) soft brown sugar
60 g (2 oz) sultanas
25 g (1 oz) currants
150 ml (¼ pint) skimmed milk
1 heaped tablespoon malt extract
1 level tablespoon golden syrup
low-fat cooking spray

1 Preheat the oven to Gas Mark 3/ 160°C/fan oven 140°C. Put the flour, sugar, sultanas and currants in a large mixing bowl.
2 Warm the milk, malt extract and syrup together in a small pan and blend them together.
3 Pour the liquid into the bowl containing the dry ingredients then mix well.
4 Spray a 450 g (1 lb) loaf tin with low-fat cooking spray.
5 Put the mixture in the tin then smooth it over with a little hot or warm water. Bake in the middle of the oven for 45 minutes–1 hour.
6 Leave to cool before turning out. When cold, wrap the loaf in foil or clingfilm. Leave for a day before slicing.

BANANA AND FIG LOAF

POINTS

| per recipe: $29^{1/2}$ | per slice: 3 |

V *Makes 10 slices*
Preparation time: 15 minutes + 20 minutes soaking + cooling
Cooking time: 1 hour
Calories per slice: 205
Freezing: not recommended

A delicious loaf for the anniversary cookbook suggested by Mary Olsen, a Leader from Cramlington.

150 g (5½ oz) All Bran
200 ml (7 fl oz) skimmed milk
100 g (3½ oz) fructose
1 egg, beaten
100 g (3½ oz) no-soak dried figs, chopped
2 small bananas, mashed
1 teaspoon ground nutmeg
50 g (1¾ oz) sultanas
175 g (6 oz) self-raising white flour

1 Place the All Bran in a large bowl and pour the milk over. Stir well and leave to stand for 20 minutes.
2 Preheat the oven to Gas Mark 4/ 180°C/fan oven 160°C. Line a 450 g (1 lb) loaf tin with non-stick baking parchment.
3 Stir the fructose, egg, figs, bananas, nutmeg, sultanas and flour into the All Bran mixture.
4 Spoon the mixture into the prepared tin. Level the top with the back of a spoon and bake for 1 hour, until firm to the touch. Leave to cool in the tin for 20 minutes then transfer to a wire rack and allow to cool completely before cutting into slices.

TOP TIP Fructose is a fruit sugar available in most health food shops.

CARROT CAKE WITH SULTANAS

POINTS

per recipe: 43	per slice: 3½

V *Makes 12 slices*
Preparation time: 25 minutes + cooling
Cooking time: 1 hour
Calories per slice: 230
Freezing: recommended

The combination of flavours is heavenly in this moist and moreish cake. The recipe was written in 1995 and was recommended by Marilyn Webb, a Leader from Islington, North London.

125 ml (4 fl oz) sunflower oil

110 g (4 oz) self-raising white flour, sieved

110 g (4 oz) self-raising wholemeal flour, sieved

1 teaspoon baking powder

½ teaspoon ground cinnamon

90 g (3¼ oz) soft brown sugar

225 g (8 oz) carrots, grated

2 eggs

grated zest of ½ orange

150 ml (¼ pint) unsweetened orange juice

90 g (3¼ oz) sultanas

1 Preheat the oven to Gas Mark 4/ 180°C/fan oven 160°C. Grease a 900 g (2 lb) loaf tin with a little of the oil then line the base with non-stick baking parchment.

2 In a large bowl, combine the remaining oil with the flours, baking powder, cinnamon, sugar, carrots, eggs, orange zest and orange juice. Mix well until the ingredients are thoroughly combined. Fold in the sultanas.

3 Transfer the mixture to the prepared loaf tin then bake for approximately 1 hour, until the cake is well-risen, golden brown and firm to the touch. Check the centre of the cake with a skewer – it should come out clean.

4 Cool the cake in the tin for 10 minutes then turn out onto a wire rack to cool completely before serving.

Apple and sultana squares: Each square is only 2 points.

APPLE AND SULTANA SQUARES

POINTS

per recipe: 24½	per square: 2

V *Makes 12 squares*
Preparation: 20 minutes + cooling
Cooking time: 30 minutes
Calories per square: 135
Freezing: recommended

This is a fabulous recipe that is simple to make, yet really tasty. It was recommended by Jackie Cowie, a Diamond Leader from Aberdeen who says they are a firm family favourite.

2 tablespoons polyunsaturated margarine

4 tablespoons golden syrup

2 tablespoons light muscovado sugar

175 g (6 oz) rolled oats

1 apple, peeled, cored and chopped

60 g (2 oz) sultanas

1 egg, beaten

1 Preheat the oven to Gas Mark 4/ 180°C/fan oven 160°C. Grease a 20 cm (8-inch) square cake tin with ½ a teaspoon of the margarine then line it with non-stick baking parchment.

2 Melt the remaining margarine and syrup together in a saucepan. Stir in the muscovado sugar then heat gently until the sugar has dissolved. Remove from the heat.

3 Add the oats to the melted mixture then stir in the apple and sultanas. Mix in the egg. Transfer to the prepared tin and level the surface.

4 Bake for approximately 30 minutes. Allow to cool in the tin for about 5 minutes then cut into 12 squares. Leave them in the tin to cool completely before removing.

**Carrot cake
with sultanas:
A classic cake
for only 3½
points per slice.**

Double chocolate cookies: These just melt in your mouth and they're only 1½ points each!

DOUBLE CHOCOLATE COOKIES

POINTS

per recipe: 19   per cookie: 1½

Ⓥ *Makes 12 cookies*
Preparation time: 15 minutes + 20 minutes standing
Cooking time: 15 minutes
Calories per cookie: 95
Freezing: recommended

First published in 1998, this recipe was put forward by Jacqui Johnson, a Regional Manager for Weight Watchers. She says the cookies are 'easy to make, taste divine and hit the chocolate spot!'

2 egg whites
175 g (6 oz) icing sugar
40 g (1½ oz) cocoa powder
2 teaspoons plain white flour
a few drops of vanilla essence
50 g (1¾ oz) milk chocolate chips

1 Preheat the oven to Gas Mark 4/ 180°C/fan oven 160°C. Line two baking sheets with baking parchment.
2 Whisk the egg whites in a large, grease-free bowl until light and frothy, but not stiff. Gradually sift in the icing sugar, cocoa powder and flour, whisking after each addition. Add a few drops of vanilla essence. Leave the mixture to stand for 20 minutes to thicken.
3 Place 12 teaspoonfuls of the mixture on the baking sheets, leaving space between them. Dot with the chocolate chips.
4 Bake for 12–15 minutes, until firm and cracked on the surface. Leave for 5 minutes before transferring the cookies to a wire rack to cool.

VARIATION Use white chocolate chips for an interesting variation.

FLAPJACKS

POINTS

per recipe: 31   per flapjack: 2

Ⓥ *Makes 15 flapjacks*
Preparation and cooking time: 25 minutes + cooling
Calories per flapjack: 125
Freezing: recommended

A firm family favourite, these scrumptious flapjacks were first published in 1991.

low-fat cooking spray
90 g (3¼ oz) polyunsaturated margarine
60 g (2 oz) soft brown sugar
2 tablespoons golden syrup
¾ teaspoon ground mixed spice or ginger (optional)
220 g (7½ oz) porridge oats

1 Preheat the oven to Gas Mark 5/ 190°C/fan oven 170°C. Spray a 15 × 23 cm (6 × 9-inch) ovenproof dish with low-fat cooking spray.
2 Place the margarine, sugar, syrup and spice or ginger, if using, in a medium-size bowl. Microwave, uncovered, on High for 1 minute 20 seconds. Stir until the margarine has melted and the sugar has dissolved. Alternatively, heat in a medium-size saucepan until the margarine has melted and the sugar dissolved.
3 Stir the porridge oats into the syrup mixture then transfer it to the prepared dish, pressing it down evenly and firmly using the back of a spoon.
4 Cook for 15–20 minutes until golden.
5 Remove from the oven and leave to stand for 2 minutes. Mark out 15 pieces with a knife while still in the dish then leave in the dish until cold before cutting through and serving.

SPICED BANANA CAKE

POINTS

per recipe: 41½   per slice: 2½

Ⓥ *Makes 16 slices*
Preparation time: 15 minutes
Cooking time: 55 minutes–1 hour
Calories per slice: 165
Freezing: recommended

This cake was recommended by Jan Leach and Linda Clifton. The mixed spices and cinnamon really complement the sweetness of the bananas.

low-fat cooking spray
250 g (9 oz) self-raising white flour
½ teaspoon bicarbonate of soda
½ teaspoon salt
½ teaspoon ground ginger
½ teaspoon cinnamon
½ teaspoon mixed spice
8 tablespoons low-fat spread
8 tablespoons soft brown sugar
2 bananas, mashed
3 eggs
60 g (2 oz) currants
60 g (2 oz) sultanas

1 Preheat the oven to Gas Mark 3/ 160°C/fan oven 140°C. Grease an 18 cm (7-inch) cake tin with low-fat cooking spray then line the base with greaseproof paper.
2 Sift the next six ingredients into a large bowl. Add the low-fat spread and rub it in until the mixture resembles fine breadcrumbs. Add the sugar.
3 Beat the bananas and eggs together until smooth then add to the flour mixture, beating well. Stir in the currants and sultanas.
4 Pour into the prepared tin then bake for 55 minutes – 1 hour or until a skewer inserted into the centre comes out clean.

WHOLEMEAL APRICOT CAKE

POINTS

per recipe: 41½	per slice: 3½

Ⓥ *Makes 12 slices*
Preparation time: 25 minutes + cooling
Cooking time: 1 hour and 10 minutes
Calories per slice: 195
Freezing: recommended

This cake is healthy, wholesome and nutritious. Recommended by Sylvia Palmer, a slice of this cake will relieve those mid-morning cravings.

125 g (4½ oz) polyunsaturated margarine

100 g (3½ oz) caster sugar

2 eggs, lightly beaten

175 g (6 oz) ready-to-eat dried apricots, chopped

25 g (1 oz) ground almonds

110 g (4 oz) self-raising wholemeal flour

60 g (2 oz) plain wholemeal flour

1 Preheat the oven to Gas Mark 3/ 160°C/fan oven 140°C. Line an 18 cm (7-inch) round cake tin with non-stick baking parchment.

2 Cream the margarine and sugar together in a mixing bowl until light in colour.

3 Add the beaten eggs, a little at a time, to the creamed mixture, beating well after each addition to prevent the mixture curdling. Stir in the apricots and the ground almonds.

4 Sieve the flours over the creamed mixture – tip the bran remaining in the sieve into the bowl. Gently fold the flour into the cake mixture then add enough water to give a dropping consistency.

5 Spoon the mixture into the prepared tin, level the surface then bake for 1 hour 10 minutes or until the cake is golden and has shrunk away from the side of the tin. Leave to cool in the tin for 15 minutes then turn out on to a wire rack. Leave until cold.

PINEAPPLE AND COCONUT LOAF

POINTS

per recipe: 25	per slice: 2½

Ⓥ *Makes 10 slices*
Preparation time: 5 minutes
Cooking time: 40–45 minutes
Calories per slice: 140
Freezing: recommended

This delicious Pineapple and Coconut Loaf was recommended by Christine Younger. The recipe was taken from a 1998 cookbook and is a really tasty teatime treat!

low-fat cooking spray

175 g (6 oz) self-raising white flour

½ teaspoon ground cinnamon or ground mixed spice

50 g (1¾ oz) low-fat spread

50 g (1¾ oz) caster sugar

225 g (8 oz) canned pineapple pieces in natural juice

2 eggs, beaten

25 g (1 oz) desiccated coconut

1 Preheat the oven to Gas Mark 2/ 150°C/fan oven 130°C. Grease a 450 g (1 lb) loaf tin with low-fat cooking spray then line with greaseproof paper.

2 Sieve the flour and cinnamon or mixed spice into a large bowl. Add the low-fat spread and rub it in, using a fork or fingertips, until the mixture resembles breadcrumbs. Stir in the sugar.

3 Drain the pineapple, reserving 1 tablespoon of the juice.

4 Beat the eggs and the reserved pineapple juice into the flour mix to make a dropping consistency. Fold in the pineapple pieces and the desiccated coconut.

5 Spoon the mixture into the loaf tin and bake for 40–45 minutes or until risen and firm to the touch. A skewer inserted into the middle should come out clean.

6 Leave for 5 minutes before turning out and cooling on a wire rack.

Wholemeal apricot cake: Relax and enjoy each slice for only 3½ points.

Sticky cinnamon
buns: Only 1½
points each!

STICKY CINNAMON BUNS

POINTS

per recipe: 11½	per bun: 1½

(V) *Makes 8 buns*
Preparation time: 25 minutes
Cooking time: 12 minutes + cooling
Calories per bun: 90
Freezing: recommended

This recipe is wonderfully indulgent, and yet so low in points! It was originally written in 1993, and was put forward for this cookbook by Tracey White who works at Head Office and is a Gold Member.

110g (4 oz) self-raising white flour plus ½ tablespoon, for rolling
½ teaspoon baking powder
1½ tablespoon polyunsaturated margarine
zest of ½ lemon, grated finely
4 tablespoons (approximately) skimmed milk
15 g (½ oz) soft brown sugar
¾ teaspoon ground cinnamon
1 tablespoon golden syrup

1 Preheat the oven to Gas Mark 7/ 220°C/fan oven 200°C.
2 Sieve 110 g (4 oz) of the flour and all the baking powder into a large mixing bowl. Add 1 tablespoon of margarine and rub it into the flour using your fingertips. Stir in the lemon zest then gradually mix in the milk to form a soft dough.
3 Sprinkle some of the remaining flour on a sheet of non-stick baking parchment, sprinkle the rest over a rolling pin. Lightly knead the dough, just enough to make it smooth, then roll it out to a rectangle 18 × 14 cm (7 × 5½-inches).
4 Spread the remaining margarine over the dough, leaving about 1 cm (½ inch) clear along one long side.
5 Mix the brown sugar and cinnamon together then sprinkle them over the margarine. Brush the clear section of the dough with a little water. Using the parchment as a support, roll up the dough from the covered long side to the clear side. Using a very sharp knife cut the dough into eight slices.
6 Lay a piece of non-stick baking parchment on a baking sheet and arrange the slices, cut sides facing up, on the paper. Leave a space between each bun. Bake for 12 minutes, until light golden brown.
7 While the buns are cooking, spoon the syrup into a small bowl then microwave on High for 3–4 seconds. Remove the buns from the oven and leave for 2–3 minutes until cool enough to handle. Brush some of the warm syrup over the top and sides of the buns. Serve warm.

BLACKBERRY AND APPLE CAKE

POINTS

per recipe: 34	per slice: 3½

(V) *Makes 10 slices*
Preparation time: 20 minutes + cooling
Cooking time: 45 minutes–1 hour
Calories per slice: 195
Freezing: not recommended

This recipe was recommended by Jan Matthews, an Area Service Manager from Lancashire. It is a superb cake that is fruity and moist. Jan says 'it's absolutely delicious!'

low-fat cooking spray
175 g (6 oz) self-raising white flour
2 teaspoons baking powder
75 g (2¾ oz) polyunsaturated margarine
50 g (1¾ oz) ground almonds
75 g (2¾ oz) caster sugar
2 eggs
6 tablespoons apple juice
a few drops of vanilla essence
1 cooking apple, peeled, cored and chopped
100 g (3½ oz) blackberries
1 tablespoon Demerara sugar

1 Preheat the oven to Gas Mark 6/ 200°C/fan oven 180°C. Spray a 20 cm (8-inch) loose-bottomed cake tin with low-fat cooking spray then line with greaseproof paper.
2 In a large bowl, beat together the flour, baking powder, margarine, ground almonds, caster sugar, eggs, apple juice and vanilla essence.
3 Fold in the apple and blackberries then spoon the mixture into the prepared tin. Sprinkle the Demerara sugar over then bake for 45 minutes – 1 hour or until golden and firm to the touch.
4 Turn out on to wire rack and leave to cool.